DEVOTING OURSELVES TO THE PRAYERS

DEVOTING OURSELVES TO THE PRAYERS

A BAPTISMAL THEOLOGY FOR THE CHURCH'S INTERCESSORY WORK

Mark W. Stamm

DISCIPLESHIP
RESOURCES

ISBNs
978-0-88177-712-3 (print)
978-0-88177-713-0 (mobi)
978-0-88177-714-7 (ePub)

Library of Congress Control Number: 2014931701

Printed in the United States of America

DR712

Contents

Acknowledgments

When does one begin writing a book? While I made the conscious decision to write this one about six years ago, many of the ideas were stirring within me well before that. Thus, I am grateful for all of my conversation partners, some of whom I have named directly, and others who stand in the deep background.

I received valuable opportunities to present emerging insights at the 2011 meeting of the North American Association for the Catechumenate (NAAC) and at the 2011 Order of Saint Luke retreat. My colleagues in the Christian Initiation Seminar of the North American Academy of Liturgy (NAAL) offered helpful ecumenical perspectives and strong encouragement. My fellow presenters and participants in the "Leaders Living (and Dying) Baptismally" conferences held in various locales over the past two years have strengthened my understanding of the Baptismal Covenant and the missional trajectory that flows from it.

And, there is nothing like the local church. When I accepted the call to serve as a seminary professor, I grieved the loss of weekly preaching and teaching in congregations. I've never quite gotten over it. While my bishop, my dean, and my paycheck remind me that Perkins School of Theology students must be my primary teaching focus, teaching Sunday School classes, preaching and leading worship in various other locales strengthens the particular teaching voice that I want to maintain. So does my participation in the Cox Chapel and Upper Room Communities of Highland Park United Methodist Church in Dallas.

At its best, serving on a graduate theological faculty is like attending an ongoing seminar, and it also bears echoes of monastic life. All of that has helped shape this book. My Perkins colleagues and students have contributed to my thinking in a variety of ways, in feedback to classroom lectures and faculty forums, but perhaps even more, my community forms me as we pray together. I am particularly grateful for the Perkins Chapter of the Order of Saint Luke, for various chapel planning groups, and especially for those who show up for Morning Prayer at eight o'clock in the morning. Praying with you provides a continuing source of insight.

Particular thanks is due to my mother, Joanne Stamm, who proofread every word of this text, and asked good questions, often pushing me when I was less than clear. Once an English teacher, always an English teacher, or at least that's the case with her, and that's a good thing. Discussing the book with her was a delight. Of course, any remaining errors or lack of clarity are my responsibility.

Not discounting what I said about seminary and echoes of monastic life, I'm not a monk, but am now in my thirty-sixth year of marriage to Margie. This book discusses the baptismal vocation to intercessory prayer, and indeed, most of us are (at least) bi-vocational—at once spouses or partners; sons, daughters, or parents; members of communities, perhaps ordained, all baptized, all called to serve God in myriad specific ways. Margie reminds me of this dynamic almost every day, both in her commitment to our life together and in the principled way she does her work as a registered nurse. She listens to her patients, and then she listens to me while I lament seemingly hopeless first drafts. Writing books is hard work, but good work. Apart from those of us who write them, it may be that no one knows that better than one's spouse.

Introduction To the Streets and Toward the World

"It's terrible," remarked one of the sisters.

Several of the Sisters of the Precious Blood had been watching the evening news at their Salem Heights convent in Trotwood, Ohio, near Dayton. They were hearing a report about yet another murder in their city.[1] As often happens among Christians, as their awareness of the problem grew, so did their sense of call. So Sister Dorothy Kammerer said, "Isn't it terrible that we're not doing anything about it?"[2] She and Sister Canice Werner soon made a decision. They were called to pray . . . for victims of those tragedies, for perpetrators of the crimes, for children caught in the cross fire, for the general welfare of their city. Given their religious vows, one would expect the nuns to pray, because that is what they do. But their next decision took them to a considerably riskier place. Not only would they pray, but they would hold their prayer vigils on the very sites where homicides had occurred. The sisters observed the first of their homicide vigils in 1993 before a United Methodist congregation assumed leadership in 1996. Then there was a seven-year hiatus in the practice from 1999 until 2006. Indeed, such work is difficult to maintain. Nevertheless, they and various ecumenical partners have now held hundreds of vigils in the neighborhoods of Dayton, Trotwood, and Harrison Township.

The sisters were bold, but not naive. As Sister Canice told me, they needed to learn how to approach the neighborhoods, "or they would become victims."[3] With that in mind, they talked with a sympathetic resident who counseled them about how to approach their work: "You've got to know what you're doing. You must never show fear. . . . If you take a step forward, then don't turn back."[4] It was an admonition that they were soon forced to apply. On one of their first homicide vigils, as they moved toward the place where they had decided to pray, members of a local gang walked into the same street to block their path. As Sister Canice remembered it, "The gangs were as determined as we were, that we would be stopped. . . . So, we pretended that we didn't see (what they were doing). We just kept on stepping, and the only thing they could do was step back."[5] Whether or not it was the only thing that they could do, it is what they did.

Such praying is not for the faint of heart, and neither is it for the easily discouraged.

One might hope to say that the prayer witness begun by the sisters has brought an end to violence, but that has not occurred. Neither, for that matter, have two millennia of Christian praying. One cannot, of course, fully know the effect that the vigils have had on the Dayton area. More than a few have found some solace in the midst of their grief. Perhaps some have pulled back from violence, remembering the witness of a homicide vigil held on their street, or more mysteriously, constrained by a Holy Spirit whose name they may or may not have known. Some of the effects of their praying are quite visible. Ecumenical and multiracial bonds have been formed and nurtured among those who pray. Several Dayton-area churches—including, among others, Body of Christ Deliverance Center, Potter's House, Omega Baptist Church, and Precious Blood Catholic Church—are now part of the vigil-keeping community. Even so, the violence persists, as it has since Cain and Abel (Gen. 4:1-16). Rarely more than a month or two passes between vigils, and on some Saturdays more than one vigil is observed, yet theirs is not a futile practice. When the gospel is spoken and prayer offered, the violence does not get the last word, and hope is kindled among people of faith. Nevertheless, Christians must not express hope in a glib manner, or they risk insulting those who have suffered great losses.

I will return to this narrative about the Sisters of the Precious Blood and their partners in chapter 5, when I discuss intercessory prayer as our way of "standing beneath the cross with the faithful." For now, I hope you find their expression of discipleship at once impressive while at the same time thoroughly ordinary. The sisters and their ecumenical partners are doing what Christians do. Their witness points toward two particular issues that I will address throughout this book. First, they view such praying as their Christian duty, as part of the missional call that flows from their core identity as Christians, that is, from their baptism. The fact that the sisters have taken the vows of a religious order means that they have a particular call to leadership and witness, but, as they have realized, the work of prayer belongs to the whole Christian community. Second, one would be hard-pressed to say where the vigil liturgy ends and the justice mission begins; that is, if one had a pressing need to mark such divisions. While it remains difficult to determine exactly what effect comes from their praying, there is in fact an overflow of goodness, rich meaning emerging from the midst of their practice, and God is in the midst of it.

And so, the conversation begins: *Devoting Ourselves to the Prayers: A Baptismal Theology for the Church's Intercessory Work.* The title is drawn from Acts 2:41-42, which reports the immediate results of Peter's sermon on the Day of Pentecost: "So those who welcomed his message were baptized. . . . They devoted themselves to the apostles' teaching and fellowship, to the breaking of bread and the prayers." Baptism led them into a way of life that was both communal and missional, to the formation of a people who were devoted to the prayers. As the title indicates, I will discuss the work of intercessory prayer as a vocation, or calling, a practice rooted in our common baptism and shared by the whole church. I will demonstrate how the dynamics of the Baptismal Covenant itself may shape the very content and form of these prayers. In these and other ways, what follows will present a baptismal theology for the church's intercessory work.

There are, of course, many books on Christian prayer, and they continue to emerge. Why, then, do I offer this particular book? Over the past half-century, many branches of the church have made excellent progress in their sacramental theology and practice. Much of this progress came from engagement with the *Constitution on the Sacred Liturgy* (*Sacrosanctum Concilium,* hereafter *SC*), a document published by the Roman Catholic Church's Second Vatican Council in late 1963.[6] *SC* functioned like a summary document for the liturgical movement, which began to emerge in the nineteenth century.[7] *SC* expressed the church's desire that the entire Christian assembly "be led to that full, conscious, and active participation which is demanded by the very nature of the liturgy." The document insists that "such participation is their right and duty by reason of their baptism."[8] Using similar baptismal imagery, *SC* insists that "the liturgy . . . is the font from which (the church's) power flows."[9] It presents an ecclesiology that begins not with ordination and the concerns of the clergy, but with baptism and the work of the entire assembly, including the ordained.

Vatican II affected not only the Roman Catholic Church but also much of the wider church, including my own denomination, The United Methodist Church. As it was with Catholics and many Protestant communions, United Methodists moved from a heavily penitential eucharistic rite, one focused almost exclusively on the passion and death of Jesus Christ, to a more celebrative ritual that commemorated his entire life and ministry, including his death, resurrection, ascension, and gift of the Holy Spirit.[10] Moving beyond preoccupation with original sin, more missionally focused rituals for the Baptismal Covenant have emerged. More frequent Communion, services for the renewal of the Baptismal Covenant, and ritual forms for extending Communion to unwillingly absent members of the church have become regular practices in my denomination, including within many congregations committed to the use of contemporary forms. I have engaged these sacramental topics and practices both as a scholar/teacher and as a participant in various aspects of congregational life, including the pastoral role. Liturgical progress has been uneven among United Methodists and other Christians in the Protestant mainline, but it has been progress nonetheless, especially when one adopts the perspective of a half-century.

The aforementioned progress has not, however, been as evident in my denomination's public prayers of intercession. In spite of the strong missional language expressed in our revised sacramental rites, prayers of the people tend to focus primarily on local and congregational concerns. For example, at baptism we ask persons to serve Christ as Lord "in union with the church which Christ has opened to people of all ages, nations, and races,"[11] yet that insight does not shape the corporate intercessions as deeply and imaginatively as it might. When pressed with a tight Sunday morning schedule—perhaps with multiple services allotted no more than one hour each—some leaders severely curtail the time given to intercessions, sometimes omitting them altogether. In the work that I do overseeing liturgical life at Perkins School of Theology, many times I have looked at a proposed order of worship and asked the planners, "Where are the prayers of the people?" It appears that many see these prayers as less than necessary, or at least as less than urgently needed.

Why this problem? Part of it lies in the fact that The United Methodist Church offers but few written forms for general intercessions. *The United Methodist Hymnal* "Service of Word and Table I" calls for "Concerns and Prayers," but there is no listing of expected or suggested content, and further, all of the rubrics related to these prayers are "may" rubrics. That is, "Brief intercessions, petitions and thanksgiving may be prayed by the leader or spontaneously by the congregation."[12] An astute reader of rubrics knows that "may" allows one to respond, "I'd rather not," or "Perhaps we'll just skip this part today." Indeed, *The United Methodist Hymnal* provides a few short prayers of intercession, mostly in the form of collects, but it offers no full litanies for congregational use. The relatively brief outlines for "Daily Praise and Prayer" (morning and evening) provide a reasonably comprehensive outline for intercessory prayers,[13] but these are the only such outlines in the entire book, and they are just that, outlines. One would not necessarily see them as related to the Lord's Day worship of the full assembly. Thus, one could be well acquainted with the content of the church's hymnal and still not discern a proper shape and focus for the church's vocation to intercession. Without a minimum of official guidance, how do we expect people to learn a better practice?

The United Methodist Book of Worship (*UMBOW*) provides a wider array of texts for congregational intercessions, but minimally so. Its commentary on Word and Table I is slightly expanded, but primarily to include the rather vague phrase "joys and concerns."[14] What does that phrase mean, and how does it relate to God's mission? One could take it to mean that our emotional state—our joys and concerns—sets the agenda for our intercessory work. Might there be an intercessory agenda that extends wider than our particular concerns, much less our joys? While the *Book of Worship* offers no less than twenty different texts for the eucharistic Great Thanksgiving, an impressive collection indeed, its "Litany for the Church and for the World" is a section heading with but one entry, and that text is directly borrowed from *The Book of Common Prayer*.[15] One can search *UMBOW* and find other intercessory forms. For example, "A Service of Word and Table IV" includes a version of the "prayer for the whole state of Christ's Church," a classic sixteenth-century Anglican text that had been included in the previous hymnal, *The Book of Hymns* (1966).[16] The aforementioned outlines for intercessory prayer are found in three of the four services of Daily Praise and Prayer.[17] In like manner, *UMBOW* places prayers of thanksgiving and intercession among resources for some of the seasons of the Christian Year, but one has to go digging in order to find them.[18] In summary, our official United Methodist ritual texts suggest that we should offer prayers of intercession within our worship services, but there is little guidance as to how that should be done. This lack of guidance shows in our practice.

Given my position as a liturgical studies professor in a denominational school of theology, I field frequent and sometimes passionate questions about matters of sacramental theology and practice. Such queries convince me that our revised texts have shaped both our practices and our perceptions of them. For example, an epiclesis[19] has been part of our official eucharistic rite only since 1984, but if a pastor omits it these days, some congregants may be significantly troubled by the omission, even wondering if the sacrament has been validly celebrated. By and large, our pastors know that when they use water in services for the renewal of the Baptismal Covenant, they are to do so "symbolically in ways that cannot be interpreted as baptism."[20] We have been shaped by these ritual changes and will argue about their meaning, sometimes passionately. Ordination candidates can expect questions about them. In contrast, I receive relatively few questions about the weekly prayer of the faithful, nor do I hear much about Boards of Ordained Ministry quizzing ordination candidates as to their views on the leadership of intercessory prayers, their content and proper shape. While there are some exceptions, the prayer of the faithful appears to be a matter of relative indifference to us; but such is the case not only among United Methodists. Even in denominations with ample strong texts at their disposal, these prayers are often used with little imagination or attempt to respond to emerging circumstances. In many cases, their leaders rush through them on the way to the Eucharist.

My point here is that congregations should care about our intercessory work far more than they have. Given the deficiencies that I have described here, I have committed myself to improving and deepening the practice of these prayers. When that conviction first began to emerge for me, I thought that my scholarship and teaching were moving in an entirely new direction, away from the questions of sacramental theology and practice that had characterized my previous work. To my delight, however, I rediscovered that strong biblical and historical connection between baptism and this work of praying for others, a connection that I have already begun to discuss here.[21] I will take up that discussion at length in chapter 2, pointing to several key historical sources, and raising questions about what they mean for contemporary Christians. I will urge us to see the connection not in terms of access but in terms of vocation; not in terms of who gets to pray and who does not, but in terms of a compelling urgency. Intercession is that which the baptized must do, and we take up that assignment at the font.

In chapter 3 I will point to the work of some contemporary practitioners—not prominent theologians but church members and pastors—asking how one embodies such a vocation to prayer. Having looked at some exemplars, in chapter 4 I will ask how the church might form others to pray in a similar manner. In various ways, these two chapters raise a question that must remain central to liturgical theology: What does a particular practice look like? That question was never far from my mind in my previous work, and it will remain close at hand in this investigation.

In chapters 5 and 6, I will take up two central dynamics of the Baptismal Covenant, asking how they might inform us for the shaping of the church's intercessions. Reflecting upon the New Testament assertion that we are baptized into the death of Jesus Christ (Rom. 6:3-4), in chapter 5 I will examine intercession as direct encounter with human suffering, as it were, our standing under the cross attending to the suffering Christ. In chapter 6, I will take up the baptismal dynamic of *metanoia* (or change of mind, a turn in another direction), a word usually translated as "repentance" or "repent." I will urge us to see metanoia not primarily as a negative movement, but as a hopeful turning toward the reign of God (Matt. 3:2). Intercession is one way for us to participate in that turning.

In chapter 7, I will discuss the community of the baptized not only as those who pray together during Sunday mornings and at other liturgical gatherings, but also as those who should participate in discerning the very shape of the prayers that their community offers. Here I will suggest engaging in a conversation that centers around the open-ended question, Why don't we pray for . . . ?

In the final chapter, we will look back over the discussion and inquire about the effects of offering such intercessions, asking, "So then, what difference does such praying make?" Before any of that, however, we join the first disciples in asking Jesus to "teach us to pray." That, properly, is the agenda of the first chapter. What were the disciples asking for, and, given Jesus' response, how should we follow him?

CHAPTER ONE

Teach Us to Pray

Formation in the Midst of Practice

Learning to pray faithfully is a lifelong task that involves the whole church along with all of its accumulated wisdom. Even then, it is a process that we will never get entirely right, and so we do well to remember Saint Paul's assertion that "the Spirit helps us in our weakness; for we do not know how to pray as we ought" (Rom. 8:26). He spoke this not in despair but in the context of hope. He continued, "But that very Spirit intercedes with sighs too deep for words. And God, who searches the heart, knows what is the mind of the Spirit, because the Spirit intercedes for the saints according to the will of God" (vv. 26-27). As with any spiritual practice, in our praying there is much that will remain beyond our comprehension. Nevertheless, there is also much that we can learn.

In this chapter, we will reflect on Luke 11:1-13, the Lukan version of the giving of the Lord's Prayer followed by a parable about a persistent neighbor. This passage teaches us while at the same time raising many questions. It begins with the disciples watching Jesus at prayer: "He was praying in a certain place, and after he had finished, one of his disciples said to him, 'Lord, teach us to pray, as John taught his disciples' " (Luke 11:1).

We join the disciples in this request for instruction, although perhaps with some ambivalence. What are we asking for, and why should we pray? What good comes from it? Petitionary prayer—that is, praying that God grant us our requests—can raise more questions than it answers, and that even when we are interceding primarily on behalf of other people. We remember seriously ill persons and we pray for their healing. Some are cured, and others are not. We go to the funeral of those who have died and we are not quite sure what to pray for next. Even persons who become well present us with a theological challenge. What role did our praying take in their healing, and what does that imply about our ongoing relationship with medical professionals? Would the same healing have occurred without our prayers? Is there a difference between healing and cure, and if so, what is it? Some petitions may seem blatantly inappropriate, perhaps that our favorite team win an important game, or, more darkly, that our enemies be harmed. What do we do about problematic prayers? Each of those questions is vitally important, and none of them are simply answered.

However, before we get lost in legitimate questions or horror stories about questionable prayers, note that the disciples' request emerged not in the midst of a philosophical discussion about the proper shape and purpose of praying, but rather as they observed Jesus at prayer. Even if they did not fully understand what he was doing and or why he was doing it, they were drawn to his praying. So they urged him, "Teach us your practice, and help us join you in it." We gain an important reminder here, one that points us toward an insight that we probably already know. Learning to pray happens best within a community that prays. As with most Christian practice, we teach faith by doing faith. Few are drawn to faithful practice merely through theological arguments or through exhortations to do what God demands. Our reflection on the church's intercessory work should begin where these first disciples began theirs, with the practice itself. So then, "[Jesus] was praying in a certain place," and they were drawn to it (Luke 11:1). Thus begins the shaping of a tradition.

But why pray? What good does it do? I address these questions from the center of my formation, that is, as a liturgical theologian shaped by long experience in The United Methodist Church and by my commitment to the Rule of Life and Service of the Order of Saint Luke.[1] To address questions as a liturgical theologian means that I begin by reflecting upon the traditions and practices of the church, in this case its public praying, discerning meaning from the midst of practices. While I try to observe in a clearheaded and reasonably open-minded way, I do so not as a disinterested observer, but as a practitioner myself, as one who prays, leads prayer, and receives the prayers of others.

Liturgical theologians insist that the very ordering of worship practices is significant—that is, when the various acts of corporate worship are done and in what sequence, how they are done, and by whom. Lutheran liturgical theologian Gordon Lathrop writes about the dynamic of *ordo*, the basic classical structures that occur within the traditional, historically informed practices of the church. Examples of such patterns include the classic Word and Table order, the structures for daily praise and prayer, and the seasons of the church year. Even the fact that most churches hold their primary service on Sunday morning is part of the ordo.[2] In relation to ordo, Lathrop points to the dynamic of juxtaposition, the relationship of one liturgical act to another. He wrote,

> The Sunday meeting of Christians, no matter what the denominational tradition, has focused around certain things: primarily a book, a water pool, bread and wine on a table; and secondarily fire, oil, clothing, a chair, images, musical instruments. These things are not static, but take on meaning in action as they are used, especially as they are intentionally juxtaposed.[3]

What is revealed when one changes the ordo and its various juxtapositions, perhaps moving prayers of confession to the beginning of the service, or omitting them altogether? Who decides if the ordo may be changed, and on what authority?

In relation to questions such as these, liturgical theologians often cite the Latin phrase *Lex orandi, lex credendi*, which translates to "The law of prayer grounds the law of belief."[4] Both faith practices and doctrinal commitments are important, but they exist in dialogue with each other, in juxtaposition. This claim is similar to the Anglican/Methodist understanding that scripture, tradition, and reason/experience are theological sources in dialogical relationship.[5] How does this apply to our topic? The lived practice of praying—including reflection upon those who have prayed in the past—will teach us much about what it means to pray. It is primary theology, looking back upon the last liturgy (and the ones before that), and then forward to those yet to come, with both a charitable and a critical eye.[6] From the perspective of the liturgical theologian, then, the meaning of worship is found in what it does. Admittedly, it is an inexact science, and because only imperfect people worship God, it can be a bit messy. But it is the lived theology of the church, and God is revealed in the midst of it, sometimes in spite of us.

Catholic priest and liturgical theologian Robert W. Hovda provided us with an excellent example of liturgical theology. Following the practice of many priests, deacons, and other ministers, as Hovda approached the altar, he would pause briefly and make a reverent bow toward it. That gesture embodies centuries of eucharistic theology and spirituality, both affirming Christ's presence in the midst of the Eucharists past and welcoming his presence in the current celebration. Father Hovda continued that classical practice while advocating a significant extension of it in relation to the assembly. He wrote,

> If we really see the congregation and its presider as primary signs of the presence of Jesus Christ, a simple gesture might do more for our ecclesiology and for our liturgy than a monograph on the subject. After the ministers, including the presider, bow to the altar at the beginning of a celebration, let them turn and bow with reverence also toward the congregation.[7]

Meaning was expanded and deepened with the simple juxtaposition of one bow with the other. Hovda's bow was an action both pastoral and prophetic, pointing to the dignity of the baptized—the body of Christ, every bit as much as the sacramental bread (1 Cor.11–12)—while also critiquing clericalism, the overemphasis on the role of the ordained; and he did so without saying a word. From the perspective of liturgical theology, we encounter the holy in such worship, and are changed by that encounter. Then, we adjust our living and our thinking as a result of that change.[8] The practice of praying evolves in the midst of such dialogue.

Some Reflections on the Lord's Prayer

So again, we must notice that the disciples made their request in response to the practice of Jesus. He did not refuse them, giving them (and, by extension, us) the prayer we know as the Lord's Prayer:

> When you pray, say:
> Father, hallowed be your name.
> Your kingdom come.
> Give us each day our daily bread.
> And forgive us our sins,
> for we ourselves forgive everyone indebted to us.
> And do not bring us to the time of trial. (Luke 11:2-4)

Even this prayer comes to us mediated through the communities who first received it from Jesus and the disciples. We presume that Luke was written sometime after the destruction of the Jerusalem Temple in 70 CE, and perhaps as long as fifty years after Jesus walked with the disciples.[9] The same is true for the composition of Matthew's Gospel.[10] Indeed, the gospel tradition itself shows the prayer under development, giving us two forms for it (compare Matt. 6:7-15). It has been shaped in various ways across the centuries, with various translations, with some adding the doxology "for the kingdom, the power, and the glory are yours, now and forever" and others not. It is the prayer of Jesus, but it was given to the church along with the charge to pray it, and so we have been stewards of both the text and the wider tradition rooted in it.[11] Here I will focus on the Lukan text, primarily because of the parable that is attached to it (Luke 11:1-13). As we see, Jesus commands us to make requests, but the prayer does not begin there. It begins, rather, with the hallowing of God's name (Luke 11:2).

As we are commanded in the Decalogue, we must not misuse God's name, making "wrongful use" of it (Exod. 20:7). That is, we must not invoke it to selfish ends or, worse, to harm others. Related to that warning stands the Jewish refusal to speak God's name, the unpronounceable YHWH. In that spirit of mystery, those of us who pray do well to remember that we can never fully know what God wants—"We see in a mirror, dimly" (1 Cor. 13:12); and we see God's glory from behind, and then only in a sheltered spot (Exod. 33:17-23). Therefore, our praying can seem like a stumbling in the shadows. That realization does not release us from the duty to pray, but it does encourage humility and a healthy sense of limitation. Even with our limited understanding, Jesus draws us into relationship with this Holy God, inviting us to invoke the holy name as he knew it—"When you pray, say, Father." As such, we stand with him by baptismal adoption into the triune name. Such a relationship and the prayers that arise from it are built on the solid rock of this God's covenant love and promise. This God, whom we know and trust, delivered the children of Israel from their bondage and oppression in Egypt, and so we intercede for all those who are oppressed in our day, for those held captive by addictions and abuse, even the abuse of earthly fathers. This God led the children of Israel through the wilderness, feeding them with manna (Exod. 16: 1-21) and giving them water from the rock (Exod. 17:1-7), and so we are bold to pray for our needs and the needs of others. In Jesus, this God healed the sick, and so we pray for all who struggle with illness and other afflictions. Nevertheless, intimacy with God must never decline into presumption. Rather, it should lead us to prayers that reflect deep respect for the Holy One, prayers that reflect the self-giving love that we ourselves have received.

Notice that Jesus does not call us to pray for whatever we wish—as one might address selfish wishes to a genie in a bottle—but rather to pray for the coming of God's reign:[12] "Your kingdom come" (Luke 11:2). But how do we know what God's reign looks like? Again, we know only in part, but we are learning, and we gain an emerging sense of it as we read the scriptures together. In the reign of God, good news is brought to the poor, release proclaimed to the captives, and the blind (sometimes us) receive their sight (Luke 4:18-19). In the reign of God "the poor, the crippled, the blind, and the lame" have a place at God's banquet, and God sends those who already have a seat to look for those who remain missing (Luke 14:15-21).[13] So then, we pray into a vision that is shaped by our encounter with the gospel, and as goes the vision, so move our feet.

In the next petition, Jesus bids us pray "Give us each day our daily bread," and thereby we ask God to meet our day-to-day needs. Our word *daily* is translated from the Greek *epiousion,* an otherwise uncommon word that may also be translated "our bread for tomorrow."[14] That translation suggests an eschatological[15] meaning, perhaps something like "the bread of God's reign."[16] It helps to embrace both meanings at once. From a sacramental perspective, we can say that the bread of the Lord's Supper is the Body of Christ[17] (the bread of heaven),[18] and also that it is bread of the common table.[19] We are nourished by both breads, fully so and at once. There is no need for Christians to choose between the two understandings, but rather to hold them in juxtaposition to each other. In doing so, participation in the Eucharist can help us see the sacred in every meal, and, likewise, it can help us see our sharing with the poor as related to the spiritual poverty that God feeds in the sacrament.

To join with Jesus in praying for our daily needs is not to pray in an inadequately mundane way, as if that were a child's way of praying that we could expect to grow out of as we ascend to a more mature spirituality. Such an ethereal view of prayer makes no sense as long as there are hungry persons in the world, and it fails to participate in the compassion of Jesus. To pray for our daily bread is to pray that we and all humanity receive what we need—today and without hoarding—while trusting God for tomorrow's share (see Exod. 16:1-8). As we pray in this manner, sometimes, we receive God's heavenly touch and sometimes we participate in that touch for others. Not long after I returned home from my open-heart surgery in December 2010, a colleague brought a meal to our home, two baskets overflowing with food for the day, including warm bread and even Christmas cookies for dessert. It was bread for the day (actually, for two days), and it was also bread from God's hand, both gifts at once.

Even when we pray the Lord's Prayer in a solitary place, it is offered in relationship with our sisters and brothers in Christ. Jesus bids us pray, "And forgive us our sins, for we ourselves forgive everyone indebted to us" (Luke 11:4). Prayer is less than fully authentic if it does not lead to reconciliation, to a deeper love for God, for others, and for all creation. We are placed here not merely to tolerate one another, but to care for one another, and for Christians such love must always become both specific and generous. In that same spirit, the prayer concludes with a corporate petition for deliverance, and not just for us, but also for the neighbor: "And do not bring us to the time of trial" (Luke 11:4). This petition presents a difficult and persistent theological challenge to those who pray it. If we must pray, "Do not bring us to the time of trial," does that mean that God might in fact do so, whether or not we fail to ask? Does God send difficulties upon us? To imply such a thing is to make God a monster. In the perception of some, however, acknowledging the randomness of tragedy can be even more intolerable. If a tree falls in the forest . . . what if it falls on someone I love or even on me? Such things happen more often than we wish to admit; they are perplexing as well as terrifying.

I once drew criticism for offering public prayers on behalf of the victims of Hurricane Andrew (August 1992). My critic wondered if I was praying at cross-purposes with God, who, after all, had sent the storm. He argued that I might better pray for wisdom, that we might discern meaning in the midst of God's punishment. I told him that I could not join him in his conclusion that the storm was a manifestation of God's wrath, and then I reminded him that I had prayed not only for the victims of the hurricane, but also "for those who are sick, hungry, and homeless through less spectacular causes." Had God caused these as well? I reminded him that I had prayed for both groups: "Grant them all that they need . . . especially supportive community and friends."[20] I told my critic that I had no idea why the storm had occurred, but that we pray for those affected by it because Jesus bids us do so. At the very least, I insisted, our praying for these others can lead to an increase of our compassion and also "to the intercessions of the church's hands and feet."[21]

I think I gave a good response, but nevertheless, what of this petition that Jesus bids us to pray—"And do not bring us to the time of trial" (Luke 11:4)—and the questions that it raises? They remain. In his book *Good Lord, Deliver Us: The Praise of God and the Problem of Evil*, Rowan Crews helpfully points out that the liturgical tradition as a whole does not engage in what systematic theologians call theodicy, that is, reflection on the problem of evil, even to the point of trying "to explain why an all-loving and all-powerful God allows suffering and evil."[22] Rather, argues Crews, the classic liturgical rites of the church, including its intercessions, give thanks and pray in the midst of evil and in its face, but they rarely try to explain it.[23] Indeed, Jesus did not spend much time trying to explain evil (see Luke 13:1-5). Nor, for that matter, did he receive an explanation himself both as he prayed on the night of his betrayal and as he prayed from the cross itself (see Mark 14:32-42; 15:33-34). In the end, most (if not all) of the theological attempts at explaining evil prove unsatisfying. With or without explanation, however, trouble finds us soon enough, and that in a variety of forms. Therefore, we pray, "And do not bring us to the time of trial" (Luke 11:4), and much of the church's classic intercessory agenda has focused on praying for persons in trouble, and that quite specifically. We will come back to this theme in subsequent chapters.

Even though Jesus calls us to pray in these very specific ways, we can easily talk ourselves out of it, even those of us who maintain a fairly robust faith in God's presence in the midst of the church. We may even find ourselves scandalized by the idea of such praying. "God is omniscient, and thus knows what we need," we assert. "Why do we need to ask for anything?" Or, "Isn't making requests just a bit primitive . . . potentially selfish? And really, have you watched some people pray—the gyrations, the shouting, the bizarre requests? Sometimes it's just not dignified." Some will argue that contemplative silence might be a better option, less dangerous, less messy. I do not deny the problem, but Jesus' gift of the Lord's Prayer will not let us dodge the question, as to both the use of the prayer itself and the intercessory agenda that relates to it. We are called to pray, because Jesus himself prayed, and because he commanded us to join him in the task.

"So Then, Ask . . ."

If, however, one is a reluctant intercessor, the parable that follows Luke's giving of the Lord's Prayer complicates matters even further:

> [Jesus] said to them, "Suppose one of you has a friend, and you go to him at midnight and say to him, 'Friend, lend me three loaves of bread; for a friend of mine has arrived, and I have nothing to set before him.' And he answers from within, 'Do not bother me; the door has already been locked, and my children are with me in bed; I cannot get up and give you anything.' I tell you, even though he will not get up and give you anything because he is his friend, at least because of his persistence he will get up and give him whatever he needs.
>
> "So I say to you, Ask, and it will be given you; search, and you will find; knock and the door will be opened to you. For everyone who asks receives, and everyone who searches finds, and for everyone who knocks, the door will be opened." (Luke 11:5-10)

It helps to set this parable over against the background of Near Eastern hospitality codes. When a guest arrived, at whatever hour of the day, the host was expected to provide a meal. One lost face if one could not meet this obligation, so neighbors would assist each other.[24] Seen in that light, the parable points to community, with all helping to feed the sojourner. As such it is consistent with its context in Luke–Acts, pointing toward maintaining the communal breaking of the bread (Luke 24:35; Acts 2:42-47). But then comes the difficulty. At first the friend within the house refuses to help, saying, "Do not bother me" (Luke 11:7). This part is especially difficult if we want to see the friend as the God figure, and Luke points us in that direction. The petitioner receives what he needs, but only "because of his persistence" (Luke 11:8). But why do we need persistence? Should we imagine a God who is toying with us, trying to find out if we really want what we are requesting?

New Testament scholar R. Alan Culpepper tried to resolve this dilemma by suggesting that the persistence referenced here is not that of the petitioner but rather the persistent love of the friend within the house who would not allow shame to fall on the neighbor.[25] That reading may solve one problem, but it does so by creating another—it could talk us out of praying altogether, or at least it could move us to a decreased urgency about it. Given the understanding of God held by some, asking even one time can be no less problematic than asking multiple times. In many cases it is best not to read meaning into every detail of a parable, but rather to expect one primary insight from it. In that sense, the point of a parable works something like the punch line of a joke. In the case of this parable, it should not be heard as a full-blown commentary on the nature of God. As to its punch line, there is no avoiding Jesus' call to persistent prayer. What shall we make of that calling? It is likely that we will learn its value only in the midst of persistence, and not before we begin.

Why Pray at All?

"Knock and the door will be opened" will convince some more than others, and even among the convinced it does not remove the question that we have been asking: Why pray at all? What good does it do? Returning to the parable, it helps to notice that the saying "Ask, and it will be given you" is not the end of the parable. Jesus comments further,

> Is there anyone among you who, if your child asks for a fish, will give a snake instead of a fish? Or if the child asks for an egg, will give a scorpion? If you then, who are evil, know how to give good gifts to your children, how much more will the heavenly Father give the Holy Spirit to those who ask him! (Luke 11:11-13)

This wisdom shows the way forward with a surprise we may not have expected. In his conclusion, Jesus does not focus on fish or snakes, eggs or scorpions—that is, on things requested—but rather, on the gift of the Holy Spirit: If evil ones know how to give good gifts to their children, "How much more will the heavenly Father give the Holy Spirit to those who ask him!" (Luke 11:13).

This reference to the Holy Spirit is typical of the way Luke resolves many questions. In his Gospel, the Spirit anoints Jesus "to bring good news to the poor" and "release to the captives" (Luke 4:18). In his second volume, Acts, the same Spirit given to the baptized led them into a community devoted to the apostles' teaching and fellowship, the breaking of bread and the prayers;

into a community where "wonders and signs" occur in the midst of common life (Acts 2:42-47). The Spirit formed the first disciples as a missional community and sent them in ministry "to the ends of the earth" (Acts 1:8). In these and other biblical narratives, we see a God in motion and not a God of abstract theological concepts, even a positive set of attributes like goodness, omniscience, and omnipotence. With a God expressed primarily in terms of philosophical concepts, persistent prayer may not make that much sense. But such praying does make sense with the missional and relational God witnessed in the biblical narrative. The God we read about in scripture is a God in motion, working to redeem heaven and earth, and the God that we see there does that redeeming work in and through people. Moses confronted this God and dared make urgent demands. Faced with the persistent idolatry of the covenant people, this God threatened to destroy them and start over, yet Moses interceded on their behalf:

> "Why should the Egyptians say, 'It was with evil intent that he brought them out to kill them in the mountains, and to consume them from the face of the earth? Turn from your fierce wrath; change your mind and do not bring disaster on your people. Remember Abraham, Isaac, and Israel, your servants, how you swore to them by your own self, saying to them, 'I will multiply your descendants like the stars of heaven, and all this land that I have promised I will give to your descendants, and they shall inherit it forever.' "
>
> And the LORD changed his mind about the disaster that he planned to bring on his people. (Exod. 32:12-14)

The phrase "the LORD changed his mind" (Exod. 32:14) causes problems for those who like tidy theological categories, but along with the parable of the persistent neighbor, it is part of the biblical narrative. Both texts raise questions about discipleship that we might rather avoid—for whom is God calling us to intercede, and what if we fail to respond? That question matters, even if we do not always know exactly why it does.

I can draw some parallels, however. There are members of the church who are no longer able to attend public worship who will not receive

Communion if pastors and church members fail to organize home Communion ministries. I have met such people and heard their lament. In like manner, if the local food pantry cuts back on its services, some children may go hungry. If preachers and other witnesses do not go where God sends them, then some persons may not hear the gospel. Ignorance and injustice may persist in those places. According to the God whom we witness throughout the biblical narrative, God works in and through people, and so it is with our praying. What, then, if we fail to pray? What does the world lose? What do we lose?

We do well to understand the church's intercessory work in terms of the Baptismal Covenant. At baptism we ask, "Do you accept the freedom and power God gives you to resist evil injustice, and oppression in whatever forms they present themselves?"[26] According to the rite, a major part of our missional task is this ongoing work of resisting evil; in the power of the Spirit working with God to roll back the darkness and despair that continue to threaten us. As we intercede for others, we join God in that work. As we have said, we learn what it means and what good it does primarily by immersing ourselves in the process and then reflecting on our experience.

What about Christ's presence in the midst of the body of Christ, the community of the baptized? How is Christ present in and through the intercessions offered by that body? There has been long and historic controversy over the precise nature of Christ's presence within the church's celebration of the Eucharist. As we know quite well, with the hardening of these positions came anathemas and other harsh words toward Christians with contrary positions. In our contemporary celebrations, however, there exists more of a spiritual consensus than we may realize. For example, with our renewed ritual forms, Catholics, United Methodists, and Christians of other churches now pray a strong epiclesis within their respective eucharistic prayers. How does God answer that petition? Of course, significant differences remain on that particular question, and these must be taken seriously; but even then, the metaphysical reality of Christ's presence will always exceed our ability to describe it. Many of us—Protestant, Catholic, and Orthodox—will proclaim that Christ is made known to us in the breaking of the bread (Luke 24:35), and the effects of that encounter are made visible in the deepened love and justice of sanctified lives. If Christ is made known to us in the Eucharist, then it is not a particularly strenuous extension of logic to believe that he is also active within the body of Christ as it intercedes through him, with him, and in him.

CHAPTER TWO

Living Water from the Font

Baptism and the Vocation to Intercession

What happens when we are baptized? Taking the question one step further, what does God intend for those who have received it, for those who live within the Baptismal Covenant? Because God is at work in the sacraments, one can never answer that question in a fully definitive way, and there will always be more to the sacraments than we can comprehend. On the other hand, God has chosen to reveal God's self to us—and our experience of that revelation continues—so there is much about baptism that we can affirm. In and through baptism, we are called to repentance, and we receive the forgiveness of sins (Mark 1:4; Acts 22:16). Through baptism, we receive the gift of the Holy Spirit, receiving a new birth in water and spirit (John 3:5-7; Acts 2:38). In baptism, we receive God's covenant promise, a promise that extends not only to us, but also to our children and to generations yet unborn (Acts 2:39). Through baptism, the Spirit makes us part of the body of Christ, the church, uniting us with Jesus Christ and giving us a new multiethnic, multinational family (1 Cor. 12:12-13; Rom. 6:3-5; Gal. 3:27-29). In baptism, a fundamental (ontological)[1] change occurs in our very being; thus one is not the same person following baptism that one was before it occurred. How could a person be united to Christ and remain the same?[2]

In baptism, one inherits the family history of the covenant people of God; or, as my denomination expresses it, "Through the Sacrament of Baptism . . . we are incorporated into God's mighty acts of salvation."[3] Through baptism, then, one enters the newest chapter of an ancient narrative, and one becomes an active part of it.[4]

Baptism saves us (Acts 2:40; 1 Pet. 3:21). Although that claim is biblical, it invariably sparks controversy, and, indeed, it should push us to reevaluate what we mean when we use words like *salvation* and *saved.* When we assert that baptism saves us, are we claiming that the baptized are guaranteed a place in heaven after they die, regardless of whether they have lived faithfully? If so, what sense can we make of God's commandments and the call to love and justice? Perhaps worse, are we saying that those who did not receive baptism are condemned to eternal punishment, even faithful adherents of other religions and children of Christians who die before receiving baptism? There is good reason to avoid speculation on the judgment of God and the divine motivation for it, because we sinners invariably have made a mess of such speculations, sometimes tragically so. If I discuss judgment at all, much less try to administer it, I want to tread lightly and with abundant mercy, lest I be judged also, the log in my eye clouding my vision of the speck in another's eye (Matt. 7:1-5). Along with the church, I believe that Jesus Christ "will come again to judge the living and the dead,"[5] and even now we may experience that judgment, although if it is God's judgment, it is always mixed with mercy and hope. Even with belief in God's judgment, we must never underestimate the range of God's mercy, which far exceeds our ability to perceive it.

Given that understanding, it is difficult for me to imagine the Father of our Lord Jesus Christ condemning someone, adult or child, simply because they had not been baptized. Such an understanding reduces baptism to something like a magical talisman or eternal fire insurance policy, and it reduces our understanding of Christian faith to something like an exclusive club for the conventionally pious, with a clearly defined set of insiders and outsiders. Again, that does not sound like the biblical narrative in which God formed a covenant people, promising to bless the earth through them (Gen. 12:1-3; Acts 1:8). Baptism, indeed salvation, is about much more.

Unfortunately, much of the church's historic teaching has encouraged us to view baptism, and thereby, salvation, in an individualistic manner, focused on questions of one's eternal destiny. Perhaps the biggest problem has been the linking of baptism to the doctrine of original sin. The latter doctrine developed for good reason, as rejection of the idea that one could live in a faithful manner apart from the grace of God. Whether one acknowledges God or not, we can rejoice in all instances where love, mercy, and justice are made known, because we believe that God is at work in such dynamics. All is grace. Without the understanding of human limitation expressed in the doctrine of original sin, however, arrogance can take hold even among believers, and persons may come to believe that the reformation of the world is entirely up to them. Amid such a delusion, they set out to change it in their own power, often violently, and according to their own whims. A significant theological challenge arose, however, when the doctrine of original sin became linked with notions of guilt and punishment. Original sin came to describe not only one's inability to do good apart from God, but also an inherited state of guilt for which one was accountable even unto punishment, even in the case of newly born children. Baptism was viewed as the remedy for this guilt. Augustine of Hippo (354–430) made the following connections between original sin, inherited guilt, and baptism:

> 42. This is the meaning of the great sacrament of baptism, which is celebrated among us. All who attain to this grace thereby die to sin—as (Christ) himself is said to have died to sin because he died in the flesh, that is, "in the likeness of sin"—and they are thereby alive by being reborn in the baptismal font, just as he rose again from the sepulcher. This is the case no matter what the age of the body.
>
> 43. For whether it be a newborn infant or a decrepit old man—since no one should be barred from baptism—just so, there is no one who does not die to sin in baptism. Infants die to original sin only; adults, to all those sins which they have added, through their evil living, to the burden they have brought with them at birth. . . .

> 46. It is also said—and not without support—that infants are involved in the sins of their parents, not only of the first pair, but even of their own, of whom they were born. Indeed that divine judgment, "I shall visit the sins of the fathers on their children," definitely applies to them before they come into the New Covenant by regeneration. . . .
>
> This is why each one of them must be born again, so that he may thereby be absolved of whatever sin was in him at the time of birth. For the sins committed by evil-doing after birth can be healed by repentance. . . .
>
> 47. But in the matter of one's other parents, those who stand as one's forebears from Adam down to one's own parents, a question might well be raised: whether a man at birth is involved in the evil deeds of all his forebears. . . . God threatens to visit the sins of the parents as far as—but no further than—the third and fourth generations, because in his mercy he will not continue his wrath beyond that. It is not his purpose that those not given the grace of regeneration be crushed under too heavy a burden in their eternal damnation, as they would be if they were bound to bear, as original guilt, all the sins of their ancestors from the beginning of the human race, and to pay the due penalty for them.[6]

In his view, all are born guilty and liable for the same. This position continued to drive baptismal practice in the Western church, holding even unto the sixteenth-century Reformation and beyond, with the Anabaptist movement as the primary exception. For instance, John Wesley's position, expressed in the mid-eighteenth-century treatise *On Baptism*,[7] echoes the teaching of the Church of England, which in turn echoes that of Augustine. As to the benefits of baptism, Wesley's *On Baptism* states,

> The first of these is the washing away the guilt of original sin by the application of the merits of Christ's death. That we are all born under the guilt of Adam's sin and that all sin deserves eternal misery was the unanimous sense of the ancient Church as it was expressed in the ninth Article of our own.[8]

Baptism, insisted Wesley, is the remedy for this sin and guilt. And so, he continued as follows:

> Agreeably to this, our Church prays in the baptismal office that the person to be baptized may be "washed and sanctified by the Holy Ghost, and being delivered from God's wrath, receive remission of sins and enjoy the everlasting benediction of his heavenly washing."[9]

Indeed, this understanding of original sin and its relationship to baptism and salvation continues to drive baptismal practice in our day, even for those who argue against the baptism of children. Many of them will argue, How can baptism save a child who has never professed Christ?

What would happen, however, if we were to understand salvation, and thus baptism, in a different way, according to an expanded paradigm? Given that the discussion of heaven (and, for that matter, hell) is a relatively minor topic throughout the scriptures, it is odd for us to view salvation primarily as a matter of where one will spend eternity, but we can arrive at a better understanding. Throughout scripture, God's saving intention is repeatedly expressed in terms of blessing and redeeming the world. God called Abraham and formed the covenant people that they might be a blessing to the whole world (Gen. 12:1-3), and the church was given a similar promise and charge, to carry the gospel witness "to the ends of the earth" (Acts 1:8). Salvation looks like a peaceable kingdom, where "the wolf shall live with the lamb" (Isa. 11:6), where a great feast is spread and tears are dried (Isa. 25:6-8):

> It will be said on that day,
> Lo, this is our God; we have waited for him, so that he might save us.
> This is the Lord for whom we have waited;
> Let us rejoice and be glad in his salvation. (Isa. 25:9)

Salvation is streams in the desert, the opening of the eyes of the blind, and the leaping and dancing of the lame (Isa. 35:1-10; Matt. 11:2-6; Acts 3:1-10). The final vision of salvation in the New Testament is not about individuals going to heaven but rather about the new heaven and the new earth "coming down out of heaven from God" (Rev. 21:2). It envisions the renewal and renovation of this world, and not our escape from it. Even the mystery of resurrection, as presented in the Gospel narratives, is not about escape from earth to some promised ethereal place. The disciples eat with the risen Christ and with one another, and they are given a mission to forgive sins and love one another (Luke 24:13-35; John 20:19-31; 21:15-21). Resurrection looks to the transformation of our bodies (1 Cor. 15). Indeed, resurrection assures us that our individual personal futures rest in God's hand, and thus we need not worry about them: "If for this life only we have hoped in Christ, we are of all people most to be pitied" (1 Cor. 15:19). While the specific details of that future remain a mystery held by God, from whose love we cannot be separated (1 Cor. 15:51-57; Rom. 8:35-39), God saves us now, in and for this life, and not just in the future. Indeed, Paul completed his exhortation about belief in resurrection by pointing the faithful toward their Christian vocation, toward their work: "Therefore, my beloved, be steadfast, immovable, always excelling in the work of the Lord, because you know that in the Lord your labor is not in vain" (1 Cor. 15:58). And the work of the Christian, whatever its particular shape, must be about loving the neighbor. From another perspective, then, ours is not to stand "looking up toward heaven," but rather to await the promise of God, who leads us into mission (Acts 1:8, 11, and the rest of the book to its completion).

So, yes, baptism saves us, not by somehow coaxing (or forcing) God to be merciful to us, and not primarily by canceling an inherited debt and assuring us an eternity in heaven. As noted earlier, God works an ontological change in us at baptism, one that we cannot full describe. And yes, baptism addresses the problem of sin, but in ways that transcend an individualistic understanding of it. God saves us baptismally by grafting us onto the covenant people and their narrative, by placing us among a people where the means of grace abound. Indeed, we cannot live virtuously by ourselves, and so God places us among people who receive the Eucharist and attempt (by grace) to live in a eucharistic manner. These baptized people live with new focus, including the calling to intercede on behalf of the world. That they do so haltingly does not mean that grace is frustrated or their witness is in vain. According to this understanding, our salvation comes in deliverance from our individual preoccupations and our subsequent participation in God's mission. We become part of what God is doing in the world, indeed, in all creation. Such salvation does not, of course, happen all at once, but it occurs over time as we are shaped in the gracious process that Wesleyans and other Christians call sanctification.

So then, baptism places one amid the community of those who receive the Eucharist and are called to live into the eucharistic vision. This connection between baptism and receiving Communion has been much explored in recent years, and not without controversy. Within the last decade and a half, United Methodists,[10] Presbyterians,[11] and Episcopalians,[12] among others, have taken up discussions about Communion for the nonbaptized, sometimes called open Communion, coming to differing conclusions on the topic. None of them, by the way, have been particularly effective in halting the practice within local congregations. As I argued in my book *Let Every Soul Be Jesus' Guest: A Theology of the Open Table*, we need to understand the classic ordo of baptism leading to Eucharist while also gaining an understanding of what shapes and motivates the practice of churches who give Communion to those who have not been baptized. I argued that such an open table should be viewed as an exception to the classic ordo.[13] The witness of St. Gregory of Nyssa Episcopal Church and its Director of Ministry, Sara Miles, stands over against both those who assert the norm and those who, like myself, assert it but allow for exceptions to the norm. According to Miles, she wandered in off the street one Sunday, received Communion at their open table, and experienced a dynamic conversion. She wrote, "Jesus happened to me,"[14] and who can dispute the evidence? Again, it is a much-discussed topic.

In contrast, however, relatively little has been made of similar connections between baptism and the common work of intercessory prayer.[15] In particular, there has not been any noticeable controversy about persons who pray with congregations prior to their baptism. Nevertheless, the textual evidence is just as strong for this connection as it is for the other, and thus the primary thesis for this chapter: There is an essential connection between baptism and the Christian work of intercessory prayer, and that connection should be understood in terms of vocation, as participation in God's mission. I will provide textual evidence to support this claim, using a variety of ancient sources. I will do so beginning with the story of the church's first Pentecost, recounted in the second chapter of Acts. In all likelihood, you know the story well; but allow yourself to hear it again, this time as a baptismal narrative that speaks to the formation of Christian disciples. Considering the question with which I began this chapter, note what happened to them when they were baptized.

Acts 2: Baptism and "The Prayers"

The narrative begins with the followers of Jesus "all together in one place" (Acts 2:1), in Jerusalem, where they were awaiting the promised gift of the Holy Spirit (Acts 1:4-5), which came in "a sound like the rush of a violent wind" (Acts 2:2) and filled their gathering place. These disciples were "filled with the Holy Spirit and began to speak in other languages, as the Spirit gave them ability" (Acts 2:4). Pentecost, of course, was a Jewish festival, so there were many other Jews present; these people both observed and heard what was happening, and they commented on it. Perhaps these babbling persons were drunk, they said, and given a large and boisterous festal gathering, one can imagine how some might arrive at such a conclusion. As we know, however, these others had misinterpreted the situation. Peter insisted that they were not drunk. After all, it was much too early for such things, "only nine o'clock in the morning" (Acts 2:15). Rather, he proclaimed, the observers were witnessing the fulfillment of the prophet Joel's announcement, that "in the last days" God's Spirit would be poured out "upon all flesh" (Acts 2:17-18), and many would take up a prophet's vocation:

> Your sons and your daughters shall prophesy,
> your old men shall dream dreams,
> and your young men shall see visions.
> Even on the male and female slaves,
> in those days, I will pour out my Spirit. (Joel 2:28-29)

Their prophecy expressed God's invitation: "Then everyone who calls on the name of the Lord shall be saved" (Acts 2:21; Joel 2:32).

Then Peter became even more specific, pointing his listeners toward "Jesus of Nazareth," who had been crucified in this same Jerusalem some fifty days earlier, "according to the definite plan and foreknowledge of God," yet affected through a conspiracy of Jewish religious leaders and Roman imperial power (Acts 2:22-23). Nevertheless, preached Peter, "God raised him up," overcoming death and the death-dealing powers—"because it was impossible for him to be held in [death's] power" (Acts 2:24). This Jesus, argued Peter to his fellow Jews, was the one to whom King David[16] was referring when he psalmed, "For you will not abandon my soul to Hades, or let your Holy One experience corruption" (Acts 2:27; Ps. 16:9-10). One could visit David's grave, observed Peter, and therefore the promise was made not in reference to him. It was made, rather, to this Jesus: "This Jesus God raised up, and of that all of us are witnesses" (Acts 2:32). Further, insisted Peter, in this resurrection, God has exalted Jesus to the right hand of God and through him has poured out the gift of the Spirit that they were seeing and hearing (Acts 2:33). Peter concluded, "Therefore let the entire house of Israel know with certainty that God has made him both Lord and Messiah, this Jesus whom you crucified" (Acts 2:36).

The sermon completed, what would happen next? When those who heard Peter asked, "Brothers, what should we do?" (Acts 2:37), he called them to repent and be baptized in Jesus Christ, that they might be forgiven and receive the gift of the Holy Spirit (Acts 2:38). "Save yourselves from this corrupt generation," exhorted Peter, and many who heard him responded: "So those who welcomed his message were baptized, and that day about three thousand persons were added" (Acts 2:40-41). We see here a classic juxtaposition of events, a cluster that occurs to varying extent in the other baptismal narratives in the book of Acts: (1) Proclamation and explanation of the gospel; (2) call to repentance; (3) the promised gift of the Spirit; and (4) baptism in water in the name of Jesus (see also Acts 8:26-40; 9:1-19; 10:34-48; 16:11-15, 25-34; 19:1-7). These foci occur in varying order and with varying levels of emphasis, but they are present in all of these baptismal accounts, and they remain at the core of baptismal rites, ancient, classic, and contemporary.

But the baptism of these three thousand, dramatic as it must have been, is not the end of the narrative; in this case it was only the beginning. Hear the conclusion of the chapter:

> So those who welcomed his message were baptized, and that day about three thousand persons were added. They devoted themselves to the apostles' teaching and fellowship, to the breaking of bread and the prayers. . . . All who believed were together and had all things in common; they would sell their possessions and goods and distribute the proceeds to all, as any had need. . . . And day by day the Lord added to their number those who were being saved. (Acts 2:41-42, 44-45, 47b)

The newly baptized did not simply return home, but rather they became part of a new community,[17] a fellowship (or *koinonia*/communion) guided and shaped by the apostles' teaching. We have come to know this fellowship as church. We see in this narrative the juxtaposition of baptism to "the breaking of bread," which on some level probably refers to an early form of the Lord's Supper[18] but also to other forms of table fellowship. Baptism is also connected to "the prayers," a phrase that may suggest a community pattern of some type,[19] perhaps something like the daily ordo of the Temple combined with charismatic utterances. For example, the subsequent narrative, in Acts chapter 3, opens with Peter and John "going up to the temple at the hour of prayer, at three o'clock in the afternoon" (Acts 3:1), where a healing miracle occurred (Acts 3:2-10).

Thinking in the logic of ordo, the fact that baptism led to this new fellowship, with new responsibilities implied, can be viewed as something like a vocational signpost. That is, one was baptized into a new narrative (the apostles' teaching), for participation in the breaking of bread, and for the work of the prayers; and these prayers were not merely spiritual exercises done primarily for one's own personal clarity and edification, but there was an overflow in generosity and mission, with prayers spoken then taking the form of goods and possessions shared, especially food. It was as if this progression from font to table to prayers was saying to the neophytes, "This is why you were baptized—for this work of praying and sharing, to be a blessing to your brothers and sisters, and to the world." Indeed, this is what happened when they were baptized: They became one with Christ in order to become one in Christ's mission, and that is at least part of what it meant to be saved (Acts 2:40).

This connection between baptism and prayer becomes more clear in the next two documents we will examine, a mid-second-century Roman text known to us as *First Apology of Justin Martyr*, and a text with third-century roots, *The Apostolic Tradition.* We will begin by examining *First Apology*, a text that I also discussed in my book *Let Every Soul Be Jesus' Guest*, in that case in relation to the admission to Holy Communion.[20] With each document, we will continue asking our question: What happened when they were baptized? What do the texts suggest? What claims do they make?

First Apology: Baptism and Common Prayers

One of the striking features witnessed in both *First Apology* and *The Apostolic Tradition* is the extensive processes that were followed in preparing candidates for baptism. One did not simply appear at the font or stream and request baptism—as, perhaps, the Ethiopian eunuch had done (Acts 8:36)—but one first moved through a formative process that involved repentance and fasting, learning the scriptures and a new way of life. This process came to be known as the catechumenate. As we noted, each of the baptism stories that we observed in Acts involved teaching and a call to repentance—even Philip and the eunuch had an extensive discussion of the scriptures as they rode along in the chariot (Acts 8:30-35). In the midst of that discussion, the eunuch pointed to the water and made his request (Acts 8:36); nevertheless, the processes described in these texts from subsequent centuries extended that formative dynamic to a considerable degree. How shall we hear their witness?

The Augustinian assumptions described earlier can make the catechumenate seem like a strange and foreign land, and perhaps even a hostile one. When we assume that baptism is primarily about an individual person's salvation, or, more ominously, that God's wrath awaits the nonbaptized, then waiting becomes dangerous, if not cruel. Such was the logic exercised in much of the Western church from the time of Augustine, to the point that, in some cases, midwives administered baptism almost immediately after birth, and they were encouraged to do so especially if it appeared that the child was in danger.[21] Indeed, such assumptions placed baptism as soon as possible after birth, and made the adult catechumenate irrelevant. Contemporary emphasis on baptism as a rite of affirmation, either of children or of adults, again makes delay of baptism appear somewhat heartless, albeit for reasons other than those exercised by the aforementioned midwives. Contemporary attempts to revive the catechumenate, most particularly in the Roman Catholic Church with their *Rite of Christian Initiation of Adults* (*RCIA*), have made the catechumenate a topic of some interest within the contemporary church, and its proponents must deal with all of these objections.

We should, however, hear these texts on their own terms, and then we can decide how, if at all, to receive their wisdom into our own practices. The catechumenal process makes much sense when one understands baptism not only as a means of personal salvation (or even, personal affirmation), but also, and more importantly, as entrance into a new set of responsibilities and privileges. This insight applies regardless of when baptism occurs, and even in churches that baptize children, like my own, insights from the catechumenate can shape subsequent formative processes.

With that background in mind, let us hear from *First Apology*, again a mid-first-century text. It was written to explain the practices of the church over against Roman critics. We pick up the discussion in the sixty-first chapter, where we hear a summary of the formative process along with reference to the baptismal rite itself:

> As many as are persuaded and believe that what we teach and say is true, and undertake to live accordingly, are instructed to pray and to entreat God with fasting, for the remission of their sins that are past, we praying and fasting with them. Then they are brought by us where there is water, and are regenerated in the same manner in which we were ourselves regenerated. For, in the name of God, the Father and Lord of the

> universe, and of our Saviour Jesus Christ, and of the Holy Spirit, they then receive the washing with water.[22]

Justin then embarks on a series of arguments with both Jewish and pagan opponents, which need not trouble us here.[23] In chapter 65 he returns to his community's baptismal ordo, and this is our concern. In particular, pay careful attention to that which occurs immediately following the baptism of the new Christians:

> But we, after we have thus washed him who has been convinced and has assented to our teaching, bring him to the place where those who are called brethren are assembled, in order that we may offer hearty prayers in common for ourselves and for the baptized [illuminated] person, and for all others in every place, that we may be counted worthy, now that we have learned the truth, by our works also to be found good citizens and keepers of the commandments . . .[24]

As we saw in the sixty-first chapter, there is some mention of the candidates praying during that period leading to their baptism. It seems, however, that it was focused primarily on their personal preparation for the font, that is, "[entreating] God . . . for the remission of their sins that are past."[25] Following baptism, however, the focus and scope of their praying changed. First, they moved to a new place, to the gathering of the entire baptized assembly. They still prayed for themselves, but now also for their fellow Christians and "for all others in every place."[26] The latter is an intriguing, wonderfully open-ended phrase. We can only speculate as to what such intercessions included, but one can imagine them varying and deepening over time, with extended reach. Notice another intriguing phrase related to the postbaptismal praying. They prayed and served others that they may "be found good citizens and keepers of the commandments."[27] Their praying was an expression of their citizenship within God's household, that is, of their calling to serve. Their baptism had initiated them into that citizenship, with both its blessings and its responsibilities.

First Apology continues the description of their postbaptismal ordo, expressing the much-discussed connection between baptism and admission to Communion:

> Having ended the prayers, we salute one another with a kiss. Then is brought to the president of the brethren bread and a cup of wine mixed with water; and he taking them gives praise and glory to the Father of the universe . . . and offers thanks at considerable length for our being counted worthy to receive these things at His hands. . . .
>
> And this food is called among us *Eucharistía* [the Eucharist], of which no one is allowed to partake but the man who believes that the things which we teach are true, and who has been washed with the washing that is for the remission of sins and unto regeneration, and who is living as Christ has enjoined.[28]

Indeed, one finds here a clear statement that prohibits giving communion to the unbaptized, and it is not the first time such a prohibition appears in the literature. *Didache*, a late first- or early second-century document, had said, "You must not let anyone eat or drink of your Eucharist except those baptized in the Lord's name. For in reference to this the Lord said, 'Do not give what is sacred to dogs.' "[29] *First Apology* offers no such prohibition in relation to the prayer of the assembly, but the next text we will examine does so. How shall we understand both of these prohibitions?

The Apostolic Tradition and "Not Praying with the Faithful Until . . ."

Once thought the product of a third-century Roman bishop named Hippolytus,[30] contemporary scholarship now considers *The Apostolic Tradition* (hereafter, *AT*) a composite document that developed over several centuries, with parts of it dating to the third century and perhaps earlier.[31] *AT* presents us with a highly developed catechumenal process that began with a strong examination that demanded an immediate and decisive repentance from those who presented themselves. For example, gladiators, prostitutes, and idol makers, among others, were told to cease these pursuits, and if they would not do so, they were sent away.[32] An individual could spend as long as three years in the formative work of the catechumenate.[33] As in *First Apology*, persons who had not been baptized were forbidden to receive Holy Communion: "Do not let the catechumens sit at the supper of the Lord with the faithful."[34]

Concerning our investigation of the baptismal ordo and the church's intercessory work, the most significant part of the text occurs following the postbaptismal anointing[35] and continuing to the beginning of the Eucharist. Here is a translation from the Latin text of *AT*, chapter 21, as provided in the work of Paul F. Bradshaw, Maxwell E. Johnson, and L. Edward Phillips:

> (23) And signing [him] on the forehead, let him offer [him] a kiss and let him say, "The Lord [be] with you." And let him who has been signed say, "And with your spirit."
>
> (24) Let him do thus to each one.
>
> (25) And afterward let them then pray together with all the people, not praying with the faithful until they have carried out all these things.
>
> (26) And when they have prayed, let them offer the peace with the mouth.
>
> (27) And then let the oblation be presented by the deacons to the bishop and let him give thanks (over) the bread for the representation (which the Greek calls antitype) of the body of Christ; [and over] the cup mixed with wine for the antitype (which the Greek calls "likeness") of the blood that was shed for all who have believed in him.[36]

Here one finds a clear prohibition expressed in relation to the corporate prayers of the assembly. According to the text, one did not join in those prayers until after baptism and anointing, in the same way that one did not participate in the Eucharist before receiving baptism. As I discovered in my research on open Communion practices, many contemporary Christians will read such prohibitions as exclusionary, and therefore will view them in negative terms.[37] For reasons both practical and theological, I am in no way advocating that we exclude the nonbaptized from our intercessory work. Let prayers arise from all creation, including the groaning of all things living (Rom. 8:18-27; Ps. 148). God is compassionate far beyond our comprehension, and if there needs to be any sifting or sorting of our intercessions, God will handle it.

Having said that, however, how can we hear the witness of *The Apostolic Tradition* and receive its positive intent? The best reading of this baptismal ordo is not to focus on what catechumens could not do before baptism, for in doing so we may impose our contemporary political and spiritual agenda upon the text. Rather, we should focus our attention on what all Christians were expected to do following baptism. As with *First Apology*, the first thing that the new Christians did following baptism was to join the community for prayers on behalf of others, thus taking on a responsibility in which they were expected to continue for the rest of their lives. Besides this witness to prayer found within its baptismal ordo, *AT* charged the faithful to follow a daily round of praying that was to begin each day as soon as they awoke and continue at set intervals throughout the day: "The believers, at the time when they awake and get up, before they work at anything, should pray to the Lord, and after that turn to their labors."[38]

Once again, one should read the baptismal ordo in *AT* as a vocational marker indicating that the work of intercession is the responsibility of the baptized, as well as their high privilege. One can read the classic eucharistic ordo along the same spiritual and theological trajectory—that the work of the baptized is not only to receive Communion and its benefits, but also to become a living sacrifice given and poured out for the benefit of the world (Rom. 12:1-2; Mark 10:35-40). As I have argued earlier, that is part of the benefit of receiving Communion; through sacramental participation God thus saves us from preoccupation with our own concerns, and we are freed for the self-giving for which God created all humanity.

Beyond the Ancient Baptismal Ordo: Vocational Signposts Remaining

With the emergence of Christendom and the predominance of infant baptism, the prebaptismal formational disciplines witnessed in the ancient catechumenate fell into disuse. Even with that decline, however, ritual connections between baptism and the Christian vocation to prayer remained. As J. D. C. Fisher describes it in his *Christian Initiation: Baptism in the Medieval West*, in the Gelasian Sacramentary (oldest manuscript, eighth century), the Creed was delivered to the infant candidate prior to baptism, along with the Lord's Prayer, just as had been done in some forms of the ancient catechumenate. How so, given that the candidates were infants? Acolytes would hold the infants while reciting the Creed on their behalf, and a deacon recited the Lord's Prayer.[39] The interval between delivery of the Creed and the prayer and its recitation had essentially disappeared, but the ritual connection between baptism and prayer remained, if only in vestigial form. In the Sarum Missal, the Catholic rite in England originating in the eleventh century and in use immediately prior to the Reformation (sixteenth century), the godparents said the Lord's Prayer, the Hail Mary, and the Apostles' Creed on behalf of the infant baptismal candidate.[40] These recitations were followed immediately by the blessing of the font and then the baptism of the child.[41] This ritual juxtaposition is a vestige of the ancient ordo, and once again, it expresses the vocational connection between baptism and prayer.

The Sarum rite heavily influenced the baptism and confirmation rites in The Book of Common Prayer (hereafter BCP), which contained the ritual texts of the English Reformation, and was the first liturgical book in English. We will now turn to the relevant portions of the 1549 BCP, [42] which maintains clear vestiges of the ancient juxtaposition between font and prayer.

Baptismal Vocation to Prayer as Expressed in The Book of Common Prayer

As the Reformation developed, the motivation for baptism remained much the same as it had been before it began: It was the remedy for original sin. This assumption was clearly expressed in the opening words of the baptismal rite:

> Dear beloved, for as much as all men be conceived and born in sin, and that no man born in sin, can enter into the kingdom of God (except he be regenerate and born anew of water, and the Holy Ghost) I beseech

> you to call upon God the Father through our Lord Jesus Christ, that of his bounteous mercy he will grant to these children that thing, which by nature they cannot have, that is to say, they be baptized with the Holy Ghost, and received into Christ's holy Church, and be made lively members of the same.[43]

The rite proceeded from the biblical warrant drawn from Mark 10:14 ("suffer the little children to come unto me" [KJV]) through recitation of the Lord's Prayer and the Apostles' Creed by the godparents, to the questions addressed to the godparents, on to the naming of the child, and then baptism in the triune name of God.

Following the baptism, this exhortation was directed to the godparents:

> For as much as these children have promised by you to forsake the devil and all his works, to believe in God, and to serve him: you must remember that it is your parts and duty to see that these infants be taught, so soon as they shall be able to learn, what a solemn vow, promise, and profession, they have made by you. And that they may know these things the better, you shall call upon them to hear sermons, and chiefly you shall provide that they may learn the Creed, the Lord's Prayer, and the Ten Commandments in the English tongue; and all other things which a Christian man ought to know and believe to his soul's health.[44]

This text reflects the Reformation emphasis on Bible teaching and direct instruction as the path to spiritual growth. The connection between baptism and prayer is evident here, both when the godparents are charged to teach the Lord's Prayer to their children, and earlier in the rite, where they continue the ancient practice of reciting it prior to the baptism itself. The baptized were called to a life of prayer, and each baptism would serve as a reminder of that charge.

That charge to the godparents then came full circle at the point of one's confirmation. In the sixteenth-century Church of England, confirmation was a relatively simple rite. Its title communicates its emphasis: "Confirmation, Wherein Is Contained a Catechism for Children." Essentially, it was an examination on the catechism followed by the bishop's giving the sign of the cross on the confirmand's forehead, along with the laying on of hands with prayer. This rubric complements the above-noted godparents' rubric from the baptismal rite:

> To the end that confirmation may be ministered to the more edifying of such as shall receive it (according to St. Paul's doctrine, who teacheth that all things should be done in the church to the edification of the same) it is thought good that none hereafter shall be confirmed, but such as can say in their mother tongue, the articles of the faith, the Lord's Prayer, and the Ten Commandments.[45]

Once again, one finds here the Reformation emphasis on edification rooted in biblical teaching, and one also finds the expression of a clear ritual connection between baptism-confirmation and the vocation to prayer. One led to the other.

Baptism and Intercession: The Ritual Connection in Contemporary Context

The connection between baptism and intercession is not as clear in many contemporary rites as it is in the ones that I have shown here, although the Catholic *Rite of Christian Initiation of Adults* (*RCIA*) is an exception. In the *RCIA* those scheduled for baptism at the Easter Vigil are given the Lord's Prayer at a liturgy held during the fifth week of Lent.[46] Their first participation in the corporate intercessions then occurs at the Easter Vigil, following their baptism and anointing with oil and before their first Communion. The first rubric for the postbaptismal liturgy of the Eucharist reads as follows:

> Since the profession of faith is not said, the general intercessions begin immediately and for the first time the neophytes take part in them. Some of the neophytes also take part in the procession to the altar with the gifts.[47]

The pattern was modeled on the baptismal orders in *First Apology* and especially that of *The Apostolic Tradition,* and so the similarities between them are quite intentional. Nevertheless, while practitioners of the *RCIA* are consistently clear that the elect are not communed prior to baptism—their first Communion is almost always at the Easter Vigil—the dismissal of the catechumens is not always practiced, so catechumens are often present for the prayers.[48] Indeed, the *RCIA* rubrics do not absolutely require the dismissal of the catechumens.[49] Thus, the linkage between baptism and Communion is often ritualized better than that between baptism and intercession. How do we understand the connection between baptism and intercession? Why does it matter?

Once again, if we hear this question merely in terms of an individual's right to access, then it seems nonsensical or even exclusionary. I am reminded of the remark made by Southern Baptist Convention President Bailey Smith on August 22, 1980, when he opined that "God Almighty does not hear the prayer of a Jew." The remark drew criticism from many, including then presidential candidate Ronald Reagan. Asked if he agreed with Smith, the future president said,

> Since both the Christian and Judaic religions are based on the same God, the God of Moses, I'm quite sure those prayers are heard. But I guess everyone can make his own interpretation of the Bible, and many individuals have been making differing interpretations for a long time.[50]

Bailey's remark was unfortunate, offensive, and completely unnecessary. It remains so today, and we will rightly dismiss it as a fundamentalist misapplication of scripture. Nevertheless, notice how even a fundamentalist framed the question as one of access. Of course, Jews can pray and many of them do so, as do many other religious people throughout the world. There is absolutely no reason for Christians to deny that fact.

While commonalities exist among religions, however, in each faith tradition prayers emerge from differing narratives and with somewhat differing goals. For instance, Christians understand that our praying participates in the priestly intercessions of Jesus Christ, which is what it means for us to pray to the Father "through Christ" and in the Holy Spirit. It would be grossly unfair for us to impose that Trinitarian understanding on the prayers of a Jew or a Muslim, much less on a Buddhist, but that understanding of prayer is essential to our practice. There need be no triumphalism here, as if to say that our way of praying is superior to the other, but there is difference among faiths and essential particularities within each one. As Christians who pray, our work is to know our own tradition while maintaining an open and hospitable heart toward all others, including their religious narratives. Christian tradition demands such hospitality. And, as we noted earlier, baptism and the baptismal way of life given to us Christians is not about who gets to go to heaven and, worse, who does not. Rather, it points us toward the particular stewardship and mission that we have been given in Jesus Christ.

Once again, when we view it in that manner, the baptismal ordo witnesses not so much to a Christian right to pray, as to a Christian responsibility to do so. We join Christ in his priestly intercession for the world, and that responsibility belongs to every Christian, and to the church as a whole. We may recognize some who have particularly focused gifts for intercessory prayer, but all Christians are called to this priestly work. We need to teach about the meaning of this connection between the font and prayer, perhaps citing some of the scriptures and texts noted in this chapter, but we need to demonstrate it as well. After all, sacraments are primarily sacred actions, supported and interpreted by holy words. In like manner, sacramental imagination is formed by strong ritual action.

Baptism and Intercession, Fonts and Living Water

With that in mind, placing the baptismal font in a prominent and visible place, and then leaving it there for all gatherings of the assembly whether or not a baptism was scheduled to occur, would strengthen the connection between baptism and prayer. Indeed, each worship service is the assembly of the baptized and its work flows in the stream of grace that begins at the font. Regardless of the architectural limitations of a congregation's worship space or the size of its font, some ritual adjustments could be made immediately.

For example, "Invitation to Christ," the study document produced by the Presbyterian Church U.S.A., suggests that the pastor lead prayers of confession while standing beside the font, perhaps pouring some of the water before or after pardon is announced.[51] In like manner, the person (ordained or lay) who leads the church in the prayers of the people could stand by the font while leading them, perhaps beginning them with words to this effect: "Let us now do the work we were given at our baptism." Or, more elegantly, he or she might say something like, "With joy, let us embrace the dignity of our baptismal vocation, as we pray for the world." Extending the example of "Invitation to Christ," he or she could touch the water while issuing that invitation.

More could be done in churches that are building new worship spaces or renovating existing ones.[52] One might consider building a gathering area large enough to accommodate the typical Sunday assembly, and then placing a suitably large font near the entrance to the nave (i.e., the large place occupied by the congregation during Services of Word and Table and other services). If designed properly, such a gathering space could also be used for community meals, coffee hours, mission fairs, and other more informal gatherings. It could even be used for funeral wakes and viewings, with the coffin placed beside the font. Beside the font, then, one would close the casket, place the pall, and begin the procession of the casket into the nave.[53] By viewing the casket beside the font, one would deepen the connection between baptism, the death and resurrection of Jesus Christ, and the death of the individual Christian who hoped in that same resurrection.

On occasions when baptisms were celebrated, the entire congregation could then join the procession from the nave to the baptismal space, all the while singing music readily adapted to worshipers on the move—that is, not long and complicated hymns, but cyclic musical structures like choruses or Taizé chants, or hymns with stanzas sung by a cantor (or choir) with a refrain sung by the congregation.[54] The presiding ministers, the baptismal candidates, and their sponsors would move to the area immediately beside the font and then others would fill the room. When the baptism was completed, the assembly could remain in that place while offering its prayers for the world. Then they would pass the peace, especially greeting the newly baptized, before returning to the nave (with more singing) for celebration of the Eucharist. At best, such baptisms would occur on unhurried, festal occasions—particularly Easter Vigil, Pentecost, Baptism of the Lord, and perhaps All Saints' Day—and they would be memorable even in their inevitable messiness. On subsequent worship occasions, persons would pass the same font as they entered the nave, perhaps touching its waters, as a continuing reminder of the baptismal grace that added them to the body of Christ, including its work of prayer and Eucharist. In like manner, they would pass the font upon leaving the assembly each week—again perhaps touching its waters—as they returned to their households and to their work and witness in the world. In those varied places, God calls them to continue interceding on behalf of others, with both their words and their deeds.

An even better version of the font and baptismal space described here would include a fountain as part of the font, with water in motion. Several ancient baptismal orders mention a preference for "living water" or "running water," that is, water in motion, likely moving streams. *The Didache*, which we mentioned earlier, gives the following instructions:

> Now about baptism: this is how to baptize. Give public instruction on all these points, and them "baptize" in running water, "in the name of the Father and of the Son and of the Holy Spirit." If you do not have running water, baptize in some other. If you cannot in cold, then in warm. If you have neither, then pour water on the head three times "in the name of the Father, Son, and Holy Spirit."[55]

Note that the author states a preferred mode, but then allows freedom to baptize in others ways, and we do well to follow him in his generosity. Although I am not suggesting that we return to baptizing in streams, there is much that we might learn from reflecting upon his preferred mode of running water.

To that end, turn your imagination to the glacier that gathers snow and ice over centuries of winters, and then slowly melts into mountain streams during the summers, blessing the valleys with clean, running water. Think about the Colorado River winding its way southwest over thousands of years, sculpting the glories of the Grand Canyon. Or think about the rivers that overflow, from the Nile to the Mississippi. On a regular basis, each engulfs its floodplain, enriching the land for the crops that follow. These and other images of water on the move remind us of the effects of the intercessory work that flows from the font through the baptized, both our spoken prayers and the intercessions of our hands and feet. They bless the world, shaping us and shaping others toward God's vision of justice, mercy, and love. Notice, however, that in each of the images I note here, the water is wild, flowing beyond our full control. We humans may learn to manage water flow to some extent, but we are foolish if we think we can ultimately control water. It is best if we learn to understand and cooperate with it. As with water, so it is with the Holy Spirit. We can learn to discern and cooperate with God's Spirit in our prayers and elsewhere, but we are never in control of God. When Jesus spoke of "living water" (John 4:10-14), he was not speaking of water flowing in pipes, but of something more like a geyser, "water gushing up to eternal life" (v. 14).

Toward the end of shaping my students' imaginations, I maintain an ever-expanding archive with photos of baptismal fonts and film clips of water on the move—streams, ocean scenes, and even swamps. My students have been enduring them while my photography skills slowly increase, but my goal is to teach, not to place my work in *National Geographic*. One of my favorite film clips was one that I shot during a visit to the aforementioned St. Gregory of Nyssa Church. As Sara Miles describes it, their font is placed directly outside the door to their nave as a reminder that one is baptized into Christ's mission on behalf of the world, and thus the font is oriented toward that world.[56] It is sculpted from rock, with the baptismal bowl at the midpoint between the top of the rock and the ground. The bowl is filled by a steady flow of water that runs down the rock, fills the bowl, and then continues down the rock face to the ground.

Photographing and filming the font was on my to-do list for my visit, and thus I did so from several angles. When I returned home and watched one of the films, I was surprised to hear a siren in the background, sounding somewhere out in the city. Since I had concentrated so much on the task of filming, at the time I missed hearing the siren; but as I watched the film, there it was, sounding amid the gurgling of the water. I do not know what urgent need or crisis that siren had announced, which emergency personnel or officers were called to duty by it, and whose lives were impacted that day. Perhaps the impact of that crisis continues even to this day. I regret that I did not stop to pray at that very moment, but that neglect reminds me of all the other sirens that I ignore. I had, however, prayed Morning Prayer earlier that day with members of St. Gregory's, a practice that they follow every weekday. As part of that office, we had prayed for those in need and those in trouble; moreover, we may believe God heard the sighs and groans (Rom. 8:22-23) of all those involved in that day's event. Whatever the details of that particular day may have been, the juxtaposition of font, moving water, and siren that I saw in that film clip represents our baptismal vocation to intercessory prayer, its gracious power, and the needs to which such praying responds.

Our prayers are like that living water from the font, flowing out to bless the world and responding to both its needs and its deepest aspirations. Including us in that work is part of what God did when we were baptized. At the end of the day, of course, the fonts themselves are merely furniture. The best example of such living water is those people of God, the baptized faithful, who take up the vocation to pray. In the next chapter, we will hear several of their stories.

CHAPTER THREE

What Does This Vocation Look Like?

Some Faithful Sisters and Brothers at Their Work

For most of us, daily response to God's call begins with the morning alarm clock. That is, the alarm sounds, we roll out of bed, and then we move toward the appointed responsibilities for that day. In my case, that means my teaching, my research and writing, my faculty administrative tasks, and the pastoral work that emerges in the midst of it all. Of course, most of us juggle more than one vocation. For parents, the first life phase of their calling begins with days of rising not first to the alarm clock—they might wish—but rather to the two o'clock in the morning cry of the baby demanding to be fed or changed. When the diaper-changing age (mercifully) passes, one learns, however, that the parenting vocation has just begun. Sometimes parents face excruciating challenges with their children, but even the routine for relatively normal children can be daunting. Consider parent-teacher conferences through Boy Scouts and youth sports leagues—with the mom-and-dad taxi service in full operation—on to driving lessons, high school band, college bills, and beyond. Whether or not one raises children, one day many of us will be called to take on a parental role with our mothers and fathers. For the Christian, all such work fulfills the baptismal vow to "confess Christ as Savior . . . and serve him as our Lord,"[1] and thus all is rooted in the dynamics of the Baptismal Covenant. Most of the time, I like my work as professor–ordained elder, and on frequent occasions I even love it. In like manner, I am committed to my marriage, my (now) young adult children and the rest of my family, and I know seasons of deep contentment and joy—even excitement—among them.

Sometimes, however, I do not feel particularly excited about the day's lecture or my students' work, that day's committee meeting or the writing task that sits before me. Perhaps I have a headache that morning or am a bit distracted by things at home, or perhaps I just don't have any particularly new insight to offer. I am painfully aware that I can be boring at times, and besides that, there is little that I can do about my increasingly thin hair. Even with these limitations, I can still get up out of bed, drive to school, and meet my classes. I can share what I have already learned, and, of greater importance, I can point to what others before me have discerned. I can show up to lead Morning Prayer and other chapel services, or, just as important, I can take my place amid the worshiping assembly, adding my prayer and praise while someone else leads. Some of those liturgies are like exquisite multicourse meals, and others more like a basic lunch of soup and sandwiches, but what matters most is that someone prepares the meal and then serves it.

As to marriage and family, sometimes my loved ones annoy me and even thinking about their needs makes me tired. To be fair, I am equally skilled at annoying and exhausting them. My wife did not particularly enjoy sitting vigil at the hospital during my open-heart surgery several years ago, especially when the procedure lasted longer than she and the surgeons had expected; but she did it because she had taken vows to stand by me "in sickness and in health,"[2] and those vows have taken root within her. God called us to marriage, and grace makes this way of life possible, even when stressful events occur, or the routine becomes a little boring. Excitement is wonderful, and it is difficult to imagine a marriage either beginning or sustaining itself without it, yet one can hardly experience it on a daily basis.

I am a bit suspicious of those who think that life can be endlessly entertaining. I have come to believe, rather, that maintaining a routine of steady commitment—something akin to showing up for work on a regular basis—is the key to fulfilling one's various callings. So it is with the baptismal call to pray for others. What does this vocation to prayer look like? In some ways, it looks like the practices found within the Taizé Community of southern France.

The Bells of Taizé and the Commitment to Daily Routine

For centuries, church bells have called faithful Christians to their morning and evening prayers. The tradition continues at Taizé, where large bells housed in a tower near the entrance to the community call both the brothers and the international gathering of pilgrims[3] to gather for prayer offices[4] three times a day: in the morning (8:30); at midday (12:30); and in the evening (8:30). The bells start ringing about fifteen minutes before the beginning of each service, and they continue while the people gather. When they cease ringing, the first chant of the office begins. These bells can be heard distinctly across the several square miles of land inhabited by this monastic community and they make for an impressive, memorable sound.[5] In May of 2011, I was privileged to travel to Taizé along with a group of Perkins students and my faculty colleague, Michael Hawn, who has made numerous pilgrimages there. It was my first visit. I had prepared through a decade of conversations with Michael and also by completing various readings about the community and its patterns, particularly Jason Brian Santos' book *A Community Called Taizé*, and so I knew about the bells.[6] Nevertheless, hearing about them—and even listening to recordings—did not entirely prepare me for my first experience of hearing them in person.

As with any group on pilgrimage, we had endured the typical interruptions and travel delays. Pilgrimage is, after all, a human endeavor. Even under the best of circumstances, the journey to Taizé requires one to make several connections involving various modes of travel. In our case, a delayed train had caused us to miss our midafternoon bus from Mâcon to Taizé, and thus we waited for more than an hour to catch the last route of the day, and we were thankful for it. As it happened, the bells for Evening Prayer began just as the bus arrived and we were unloading our luggage. Since we were standing within fifty yards of the bell tower, they seemed particularly loud. It is likely that the thrill I felt was an odd mixture of fatigue and anticipation, hunger and haste. We were finally here after a long journey, but the bells were sounding, which also meant that it was time to get to the Church of the Reconciliation. So we dropped our luggage in the receiving building and hustled up the pathway to the church, with the bells ringing all that time. We took our places in the church just before they ceased ringing.

The bells ringing three times a day throughout the week remained an impressive and unmistakable sound, but they also became part of the routine. Taizé is a busy place with many ongoing conversations—conversations at Bible study and small-group meetings, over food and drink, with students and others, as well as one's internal dialogue. Like any community, monastic or otherwise, Taizé is a place where routine work must be done, such as the serving of meals and their cleanup, general cleaning of the grounds, staffing of the infirmary, and, in my case, the daily cleaning of the restrooms and showers. Hospitality abounds, but no one at Taizé is treated like a hotel guest, and so each pilgrim is given a job for the week, all of it under the ready supervision of the permanents, the young adults who volunteer for stretches ranging from several weeks to several months. The pilgrims do their assigned work, and if they don't do it, it does not get done. Meanwhile, the brothers have daily work of their own. But when the bells ring, everyone stops what they are doing and they move to the church for the prayers. Following the ancient monastic tradition of *ora et labora* (pray and work),[7] the prayer offices are every bit as important as the rest of the work that is done, be it confessions heard by the prior or the cleaning of the restrooms. The thrice-daily prayer at Taizé is their way of fulfilling the routine labor of the baptized, and as with the other work, if the faithful do not offer their prayers of thanksgiving and intercession, this task may go undone. At the least, those called to it will miss the blessing of participating in it. Routine makes forgetting less likely.

A Theological Student and Morning Prayer on a Commuter Train

Many Christians keep such a routine by observing various portions of the daily office, sometimes called the Liturgy of the Hours. The thrice-daily prayers of the Taizé Community provide one outstanding example of this tradition. In many monastic patterns, such as that described in the ancient Rule of Saint Benedict,[8] it has developed into an even more extensive pattern, with as many as seven prayer offices of varying lengths appointed for use throughout the day. The following is a contemporary appropriation of the classic pattern as offered for use within my religious order, the Order of Saint Luke:[9]

- Morning Prayer (Lauds), a somewhat longer office traditionally prayed just before sunrise.
- Mid-Morning Prayer (Terce, for third hour), a short office prayed around 9 a.m., "at the hour when the Holy Spirit came upon the Church at Pentecost."[10]
- Mid-Day Prayer (Sext, for sixth hour), a short office prayed around noon, "at the hour when Jesus was placed on the cross."[11]
- Mid-Afternoon Prayer (None, for ninth hour), a short office prayed at about 3 p.m., "at the hour when Jesus died on the cross."[12]
- Evening Prayer (sometimes called Vespers or Evensong), a somewhat longer office traditionally prayed at sunset.
- Compline (from the Latin for "complete"), traditionally prayed before bedtime.
- Vigil, often reserved for major feasts, traditionally prayed in the middle of the night.[13]

When described in this full array, the sevenfold office appears daunting to most Christians, and in the main keeping this complete daily pattern has been the province of monastic communities. Indeed, my Order of Saint Luke community keeps the full office primarily when we are gathered on retreat. A more realistic daily pattern is that commended by Thomas Cranmer's sixteenth-century revisions for The Book of Common Prayer in which he provided morning and evening offices intended for use by the entire church community.[14] Many parts of the classic monastic offices were omitted and some others folded into the morning and evening services. In *The Book of Common Prayer* (1979), currently in use in the Episcopal Church U.S.A., the focus for the daily office remains on Morning Prayer and Evening Prayer, although it also provides short offices for Noonday Prayer and for compline.[15] In an attempt to encourage the revival of this more ancient practice of daily morning and evening prayer among contemporary Christians, Paul Bradshaw has argued that they were the primary people's offices in many parts of the ancient church—that is, parish clergy led the morning and evening offices, and laypersons participated in them on a regular basis. Only later did the daily office become primarily an exercise for monks and ordained persons, and in many ways that is where the practice remains.[16]

Many of us who pray portions of the daily office on a regular basis do so alone or, if we are fortunate, we have opportunity to pray with a small group of the faithful. I find it helpful, however, to remember that many others throughout the world are praying it as well, even as I pray, and the memory of participating in the multinational and multilingual prayers of the Taizé Community offers an iconic glimpse into this wider reality. Such prayer and praise never really cease. The Reverend ClayOla Gitane's story stands somewhere between the solitary and the corporate, as she began by praying alone, but it didn't really stay that way.

She attended theological school in Dallas, because at that time the Episcopal Diocese of Fort Worth did not ordain women to the priesthood. So she rose before dawn many mornings for several hours of commuter train and light rail travel, all of that in order to arrive on our campus in time for her 8:30 a.m. class. She used her time on the train to work on her Hebrew, but that was not all. As the diocesan article announcing her eventual ordination (!) reported, "During those train rides, she would say Morning Prayer with her *Book of Common Prayer* open on her lap. Over time, many of the other commuters began asking her for prayers."[17]

As she told me in our conversation,[18] for many years she had felt a call to pray the office on a regular basis. Obviously, it remains part of the Book of Common Prayer tradition even if many do not practice it. At various points in her life, she had attempted to develop such a daily office discipline, but now that she was preparing herself for ordination, her spiritual director encouraged her to try again. Given her travel and class schedule, her time on the commuter train provided the best (and perhaps only) opportunity to do so. She would board the train each morning, usually taking the same seat near the door. "At that hour of the day," she observed, "the train was not particularly full," and so she could spread out a bit. As noted above, she would place the prayer book on her lap, and then she would place her rather large *HarperCollins Study Bible* beside her for the readings. She prayed silently, reading the appointed psalms and other scriptures to herself, but her rather distinctive behavior was hard to miss. She certainly wasn't reading a novel or the morning newspaper. Over time, the other regular commuters began to notice what she was doing, and some would refer to her as "that lady who prays." As noted above, they began to bring her prayer requests. "As people got on the train, they would say things like, 'You're praying. Would you pray for my kid?' " Sometimes she would follow up with them, asking, "How is your son?" Since she did not pray aloud, there was no way for them to join her prayers in an outward and visible manner, but her practice did become a topic of conversation among some of them. ClayOla mentioned once hearing two women sitting a few rows behind her remark that it was a good idea for people to pray. Indeed so, and it appears that they were glad she was doing it.

One day a new rider boarded the train a moment or two ahead of her and sat down in ClayOla's normal place. It happens. However, one of the regular riders told the unsuspecting new person, "You'll have to move, that lady who prays sits there." Of course, we would not want a fellow church member to say such a thing to a visitor, but remember that ClayOla didn't say it, the others did, and furthermore this wasn't church. Or was it? That question aside, what matters most is how her fellow riders saw what was occurring. In their eyes, her regular seat—covered with prayer book and Bible—had become a prayer stall, from which she exercised her intercessory vocation on their behalf. They not only expected her to do that work, but they needed her to do it. Others could have joined her, and perhaps they were doing so in their own ways, even on that train; but as we rise to pray each morning we must be focused on the work that God has assigned to us and not overly preoccupied with those who have not yet responded to a call to join it. Like ClayOla, the baptized are "those women (and men) who pray."

Sometimes others understand our assigned vocation better than we do, but regardless of what they know, we must know that the world and its people are counting on the intercessions of the faithful. When deeply formed over time, that vocation can become a discernible part of one's character, and in some persons it appears in an especially striking manner. Some have told me about strangers approaching them in grocery stores and on the street, asking for their prayers. Such an occurrence could be a bit unsettling I suppose—life in Christ is an adventure, and that means it can become messy. We will return to the grocery store aisles before the end of this chapter, but next we will shift cultural contexts to look at a particularly clear corporate response to the general Christian vocation to prayer, although one must rise early in order to see it.

Early Morning Prayer in Korean-Speaking Contexts

I remember the first time I attended a service of early morning prayer in a Korean-speaking context. The first and most elemental thing that I learned is that early means early. On retreat with the Order of Saint Luke, we often pray Morning Prayer at seven, and that can be enough of a challenge, but compared to the Korean evangelical context, 7:00 a.m. prayer is child's play. My first attempt at Korean early morning prayer occurred on a chilly predawn morning in October of 2005, in the days before I had GPS service in my car. So I found myself driving on a poorly lighted exurban road, with my printed set of directions rendered nearly useless by the darkness. I almost gave up and returned home, but I persisted. After all, I had told them that I was planning to attend that day. Much to my relief, I finally found the church, arriving several minutes after the service had begun at 5:30 a.m. The preacher for that morning stood on the platform preaching his sermon before a gathering of fourteen persons, men and women of various ages, including some who appeared to be in their twenties. Among local American congregations that practice daily prayer services on weekdays, I had never seen that many persons in attendance, and certainly not at such an early hour, but I have learned that it is not untypical in the Korean-speaking context.

The sermon that morning continued until about 6 a.m., after which the lights were dimmed and the period of *tong-sung ki-do* began. *Tong-sung ki-do* means "pray aloud,"[19] and it is a good description of what happens. Of course, the whole service was in Korean, so I had no way of knowing exactly what was said when they prayed, but that's not entirely the point. When a group of people offers spontaneous prayers at the same time (in whatever language), then one can't very well obtain a transcript of the proceedings. On several occasions I have asked, "What do persons pray for during *tong-sung ki-do*?" and I have never received a definitive response. I have finally come to realize that it is the wrong question, reflecting my linear and textual liturgical scholar's perspective, and not their concerns.

In my experience of it, *tong-sung ki-do* falls somewhere between singing and speaking, with intense voices rising and falling as people offer their prayers. In some ways, that dynamic reminds me of the praying in the Spirit that I have experienced in charismatic and Pentecostal settings. The intensity is significant. According to one description, "*Tong-sung ki-do* has the character of a visceral struggle with God. Like Jacob wrestling with the angel, *tong-sung ki-do* is a form of wrestling with God. The wrestling is not just emotional and spiritual, but also physical."[20]

Indeed, *tong-sung ki-do* is an embodied practice. I have seen some remain seated for it, with others kneeling at the chancel, and still others kneeling with their faces toward their seats. Some raise their hands and rock back and forth.

Besides the early morning hour, one of the most impressive aspects is the length of the time that some of the people spend in prayer. For instance, on that first occasion in 2005, the prayers that began around 6 a.m. were continuing a half hour later when the pastor came over to me and asked if I was ready to go for breakfast. Over breakfast, he told me that some persons would continue praying until 7:00 a.m.[21] Although pastors usually exercise their teaching office at these services, the praying itself is very much the work of the whole assembly, of all the baptized, and thus pastors may leave before its conclusion. It ends only when the last person finishes praying. On one occasion that I observed, the pastor was unable to attend, and while there was no teaching that day, the prayers continued as usual.[22]

Gathering for such a prayer service is itself a countercultural discipline, especially since many entertainment options occur later in the evening. One simply cannot stay up late on a regular basis and then rise for early morning prayers, and I am told that it can take at least several days (if not longer) for one's body to adjust to the early morning rhythm. The person who commits to the discipline over time finds himself or herself in a different place, deeply Korean and, of even greater importance, deeply Christian. Thus early morning prayer becomes part of one's ongoing conversion. In this embodied way, those who follow this practice remind themselves that they are different, set apart from the world's values for a different vocation. Here again, the most important discipline may be the rising from bed and then showing up to pray with the rest of the assembled faithful.

One will hear various stories about the origins of early morning prayer, and, indeed, liturgical practices normally evolve, so they rarely have one moment of origination. In this case, many traditional spiritual practices include prayers to begin the day, and in a pre-electrical, agricultural context, one's day often began considerably earlier than it does for many of us today. Nevertheless, the account of the origins of early morning prayer given by Su Yon Pak and his colleagues is compelling. During their occupation of Korea before and during World War II, the Japanese military enforced a curfew from midnight until 4 a.m.: "At 4:00 in the morning, the curfew was lifted. It was only then that the people were free to move around and gather. For this reason, dawn evoked many meanings for the Korean people as a symbol of awakening and returning to life."[23]

And so, at that hour believers were free to gather for prayers, but in such oppressive contexts prayer is no mere exercise in wistful hope. It becomes, rather, a particular witness to the impermanence of the oppressor and his regime as well as an active resistance of the same. It remains so for all those who look forward to a better country (Heb. 11:16), and that insight applies even to those of us who live in the United States of America. As we pray, the vision of a more just world takes root in us, converting us and making us instruments of conversion in the world. Thus, early morning prayer partakes of an essential dynamic expressed within the Baptismal Covenant—the vow to resist evil in its various forms.[24] Answering God's call to pray with and for a suffering world looks like such intense early morning praying.

We will now move to the southern hemisphere, and a different time of day, for another example of a steady commitment to the baptismal vocation to prayer.

Daily Prayers at the Methodist University in São Paulo, Brazil

In May of 2010, a group of Perkins faculty received an invitation to spend a week in dialogue with our counterparts on the theological faculty at the Universidade Metodista (Methodist University) in São Paulo, Brazil. With each situated in a larger university with Methodist roots, our two schools have much in common. Our days with them were filled with faculty presentations and responses, along with field trips to various churches and mission sites across the city. We also brought greetings at one of their midday seminary chapel services. As usually occurs on such pilgrimages, the work with colleagues old and new proceeds on both formal and informal levels, and so conversations on the side and at mealtimes were among the most valuable parts of the experience. Across several such conversations, our translator—a recent graduate of their theological school and an aspiring PhD student—had learned of my research interest. Thus as our group walked back to campus after dinner on Thursday evening, he invited me to accompany him to a prayer meeting, scheduled for nine o'clock that night in the university chapel.

One of the major cultural differences between our two schools is the evening class schedule, which in their case extends much further into the evening than ours. In their case, the university runs a full schedule each weekday evening, including Fridays, with two class periods each night, the first extending from 7:30 until 9:00 p.m. and the second from 9:30 until 11:00 p.m. The prayer service occurred in that break between the two evening periods. Upon arrival, I discovered an impressive ecumenical gathering of young people, most of them undergraduates, and I learned that they had been meeting every weeknight throughout the term, including Fridays. Somewhat apologetically, one student told me that they did not meet on the weekends (meaning Saturday and Sunday nights) because most of them had church jobs; so, in essence, they were still praying on those days, but elsewhere. About thirty-five students gathered on the night that I attended.

Their short service had some affinities with charismatic gatherings that I have experienced. They began with an up-tempo song, followed by a slower, more meditative one, during which many of them raised their hands. Then came a reading from scripture and a short sermon (drawing on John Wesley's "The Almost Christian") that was delivered by one of the students. Then came the heart of the gathering. We joined hands and shared prayer requests, including some concerns that our translator had gleaned from several days of listening to our group. When I was asked to make a statement, I thanked them for their invitation, and told them that it warmed my heart to see them gathered here and praying with such commitment. I asked them to pray for me and also for their sisters and brothers in the North American churches. Following this sharing, one person led the prayer, but the others participated actively with a charismatic-like prayer hum that included murmurs of assent along with calling on the name of Jesus. While distinct, it had some affinities with *tong-sung ki-do.* Warm greetings and hugs followed the service, and photographs were taken that were soon posted to Facebook. They also shared chocolate with their guest from the northern hemisphere. I was back to my room by 9:30 p.m., and the students presumably were in their 9:30 p.m. classes.

This prayer gathering at the Universidade Metodista exhibited the energy of a typical coed gathering of young college students, whether for prayer or for any other purpose. That energy was a delight, but most impressive of all was their sense of call evidenced by their commitment to show up and pray together on a daily basis. In the next section, we will look at a woman who also prays late at night, although in a different context. While all of the baptized are called to intercede on behalf of the world, in this particular woman and others we find examples of persons with a particularly focused vocation of that work. How shall we understand such focus?

A Hospital Chaplain Nudged Awake for Prayers in the Middle of the Night, and Others with a Particularly Strong Vocation

Martha is now an ordained Disciples of Christ minister who serves as a hospital chaplain, but her vocation to intercessory prayer became evident at a much earlier point in her life. In 1996 she joined her first prayer group, a gathering of Lutheran women among whom she discerned a particularly focused vocation to intercessory work. In October 2000, God told her, "I want you to pray for people."[25] She told me, "I didn't know if there even was such a gift," although a spiritual gifts inventories taken at a later point confirmed both her gift and her calling to exercise it.[26] Although her joining the prayer group was itself a significant commitment, her subsequent discernment seemed to intensify it.

One of the groups with whom she prayed, predominantly Spanish-speaking in its membership, followed something like a vigil pattern. Teaching lasted until 10 p.m., followed by a break for food and fellowship. Then prayers would begin around 10:30 p.m., and they would continue praying well into the night, sometimes to midnight and beyond. She told me that the latest she stayed was 1 a.m., but that others were still praying at that time. As with some of the other examples that we have seen, when persons in that group prayed, they prayed aloud and all at once. She recalled, "As we prayed, I had my eyes closed and it was a very interior experience. But then I became aware that I was crying and I opened my eyes and saw that others were crying as well." She asked, "How did I know that?"[27] One cannot, of course, answer that question in a definitive way. It is clear, however, that for some Christians, a proper engagement in prayer involves significant emotional engagement, and not merely a speaking of the correct words. These and other Christians who pray passionately and persistently in the middle of the night hold much in common with ancient and contemporary Christians who rise in the night to keep vigils and otherwise pray while much of the world sleeps. These also make a countercultural move. As Philip Jenkins has described it, they are engaged in "taking back the night," that is, in bringing Christ's light to dark and sometimes fearsome situations.[28]

At times Martha's night prayers take a more solitary form, as she awakes from sleep sensing God's call to pray for a particular person in need. When I asked her to describe this experience, she mentioned once waking up with the impression that she should pray for a particular woman who she knew was approaching death. Around 1:30 a.m. she sensed that she could finally stop praying for her; later she learned that the woman had died about 1 a.m. In a sense, she had participated in transitus,[29] or, as some will describe it, in praying her sister over to the other side. Martha noted that persons with intercessory gifts often receive these nudges in the middle of the night, and they learn to act on them. Others witness to a similar experience.[30]

For example, Deborah, "normally a morning person," witnessed, "When God wakes me up in the middle of the night, I know that it's for me to pray," and so as she comes awake, she asks, "What is it?" At this point, she said, God usually brings a person to her mind, and she begins praying for him or her, even if she doesn't know exactly what the particular need may be. She said, "I cling to that verse in Revelation about prayer rising like incense, and so I pray and trust God to carry my prayer to the throne" (Rev. 5:8; see also Ps. 141:2). Deborah begins with prayers for the particular person brought to mind and then she may continue for a while, praying for others who have asked for her prayers. It was in the context of such middle-of-the-night prayer sessions that she realized, "I know that I have the gift of intercessory prayer."[31]

When I asked Deborah for a specific example from her night prayers, she mentioned a friend whose son was living with diabetes. She has awakened to pray for him on various occasions, often when his blood sugar levels have been low. In the morning following these night prayers, she will usually follow up with a phone call, and she said that it often confirms that the prayers were needed. And what, one might wonder, if such a follow-up call confirms nothing in particular about that person or his or her need? When Christians are engaged in the details of one another's lives—both their beauty and their struggles—compassion for one another deepens, and thus we come to carry persons deeply within us, in our hearts, or, to use the wonderfully telling language of the King James Version of the Bible, with "bowels of mercies" (Col. 3:12). To use Saint Paul's phrase, we "bear one another's burdens . . .

[fulfilling] the law of Christ" (Gal. 6:2). Perhaps the Spirit working deeply within us helps the subconscious mind put together the varied pieces of our knowledge and suddenly it coalesces in an insight that awakens us. Or perhaps we should simply make the bolder faith claim—that the Spirit directly awakens one and speaks a direct word. Either or both; and perhaps to say one is to say the other. Who can say exactly how God works in heart and mind? However it may occur, making a gentle and compassionate contact with a friend or family member is generally a positive thing, and so, of course, is the prayer that one offers, for God abides in the love expressed in the intercessions of both our words and our hands and feet (1 John 4:16). Moreover, God will perfect our offerings, especially those done in charity.

Our friend Martha also prays on Sunday mornings before church, sometimes for an hour at home and another hour at church "to get my heart right" before the others arrive.[32] In her pastoral role, she also leads congregational prayers, writing down the concerns that are given to her, and then combining those with the list kept by the church and printed in the bulletin. Given her deep commitment to intercession, she undertakes this task with particular diligence, to the point that one pastor complained that she prayed for "too long."[33] But how long is too long, and why? As noted earlier in the book, some churches have squeezed the time allotted for congregational intercessions down to only a minute or two. Conversely, those who understand their praying as sacred duty rendered both to God and to neighbor tend to pray more expansively, and under less time constraint. Martha also prays at the grocery store, where, she said, strangers have approached her and asked for her intercessions. Somehow, they sense that she is able to pray for them and that she is willing to do so.[34] Again, there is a mystery of compassion and connection at work here, one that we can only begin to fathom; but we can affirm that when love is present, so is God. Perhaps that is enough. Such stories take me to memories of my now deceased father, who also told stories about praying with persons in grocery stores and other somewhat unlikely places, including the local mall where his walking club gathered each morning.[35]

In his case, I don't know who did the initiating. Although he was an ordained minister, my father's sense of vocation to intercession blossomed in the years after he retired from active parish ministry. I'm not sure why this happened; as he aged perhaps he simply grew more comfortable with his sense of identity as God's child. In any event, one of my favorite stories came from an evening at the model railroad club where he was a member. When he and my mother downsized after their first decade of retirement, he sold some of his substantial model train collection and kept several pieces on display in their apartment. He moved the rest of his rolling stock to the converted warehouse where he and other enthusiasts went to build railroad scenes and run their trains together. Conversations would occur in and around such activities. As he wrote,

> Four of us found ourselves sharing stories from our earlier years. Two of the men fell into moments of confession. One said that he had been married four times. The other confessed to five marriages, two to the same lady. Then he said, "It took me a long time to learn the difference between love and lust." Then, I stepped in and said, "Fellows, this is as close to a revival service as we will ever come here at the train club, so I think we should have a prayer together." It got very quiet. I prayed, they took off their hats and bowed their heads. It was a sacred moment.[36]

He described these and similar prayer experiences as encounters with persons who briefly became members of "his parish," thereby echoing the words of Methodist founder John Wesley, who said "I look upon all the world as my parish."[37] As such, my father worked out of his long-formed identity as an ordained minister, but much of the work in those later years had little to do with the activities of church as institution or ministry as professional work. In a deeper sense, his praying was an expression of his baptismal vocation.

I love testimonies such as these and take great joy in collecting them. One encounters people and situations such as the ones that I have described here in just about every church. I think of a now deceased woman in a church that I have attended who would offer prayer concerns for particular family and church members on a weekly basis. I remember other saints, some of them homebound, who administer church prayer chains. Sometimes these people are hard to find, and it is likely that we will never know exactly who some of them are, in part because many of them take seriously Jesus' admonition to go in the closet and pray in secret (Matt. 6:5-6); when their stories come to light, however, they are impressive. I have heard some people call such persons "prayer warriors," and I have toyed with an alternative phrase, "great soul intercessors," but think it a bit too lofty. Again, these are persons who sense a particularly strong vocation to pray for others. I am grateful for their work. Who can know how many times I have benefited from their intercessions? But increasingly I feel the need to leave behind phrases that describe them as exceptional. Why so? They represent the vocation toward which God is calling all of the baptized.

This chapter's final example comes from a day when my students exercised this vocation on my behalf.

My Students Asserting Their Vocation: A Healing Service in Class

On Tuesday, November 17, 2010, I showed up for my 8:30 a.m. worship class expecting to deliver a lecture on weddings, but as I arrived my students informed me that they would be taking over the class period in order to conduct a healing service for me. Why so? I was scheduled for double heart valve replacement surgery on the following December 14, which by then was less than a month away. I had started down the road toward surgery almost twenty-six years earlier, when a physical (preceding ordination of all things) had revealed a pair of leaky heart valves. Evidently, said my cardiologists, I had contracted rheumatic fever sometime along the way, and that disease had caused the heart valve damage. Since then I had come under the care of various cardiologists, and all of them told me that "some day" I would need surgery. I had lived with that knowledge since the problem was uncovered, sometimes with less thought of it, and sometimes with more. But basically, we did an annual stress echocardiogram, and thus kept track of my valves and their condition. My diagnosis didn't restrict me very much. Since receiving it, I had served as pastor of several churches, had observed my tenth, twentieth, and thirtieth wedding anniversaries, had exercised regularly, had completed a doctorate, had worked at raising two children, had written several books, and earlier that year, had even given a scholarly presentation at the twenty-second Cooperstown Symposium on Baseball and American Culture, which was completely cool. Not long after the Cooperstown event, however, I had a less than stellar stress echo, which led to a heart catheterization. Then late that summer, my cardiologist, having reviewed all of the tests, informed me that the long-awaited "some day" had arrived. So we set our mid-December date for the surgery. Not so cool. I told my Perkins dean, my faculty colleagues, and some others, including one of my conversation partners for this project, who said, "I'll bet you didn't expect to become the subject of your own research." Indeed. Finally, in early November of 2010, I told my class, in part as a way of controlling any rumors. I asked both my colleagues and my students for their prayers but also that they let me go about my business in the meantime.

Of course, my class went about their work as well, and thus the prayer service. One of them prepared a liturgy and assigned leadership of its various parts. They recruited one of our music students to play the piano, and, further, they even brought breakfast to share at the conclusion of the liturgy as well as a baseball bat marked with a key phrase from my Baseball Berakah.[38] What could I do? "Sit down here, Brother Professor, while we pray for you." I was stunned by it all, yet more than a little proud of them. They read psalmody and other scriptures. Someone offered a short prayer that gave thanks for the healing work of Jesus. Then they laid hands on me and anointed me with oil (James 5:13-16), and, bless them, they boldly prayed for "your servant Mark," thus making no deferential and distant references to "Dr. Stamm." Indeed, I had taught them that they were not to use titles or surnames when serving Communion or doing other sacramental acts, that a Christian could aspire to no more dignified title than one's baptismal name. Deference to rank may have its useful place within academia, but not at prayer. I had also, of course, taught them that bold intercession was part of their baptismal vocation, and that leading people in those intercessions was both their privilege and their responsibility. But I had never taught them precisely how to lead a prayer service for their professor.

They also made good use of a simple sign act, giving me two greeting cards inscribed with their signatures and written blessings. I was instructed to open the first one that day, but to hold the second one and open it sometime after my surgery. And so, the second card sat unopened on my dresser top from that day until my wife brought it to the hospital following my surgery. Sitting there, it became a daily reminder of their continuing prayers, and I felt those prayers deeply. These brothers and sisters, even my students, understood the vocation to prayer that God had assigned them at their baptism, and they were bold to exercise it, much to my benefit.[39]

With this story and the other examples I have offered in this chapter, we've seen something of what the baptismal vocation to prayer looks like. Of course, you could fill out the narrative by adding stories of your own, and I hope you will do so. One can respond to God's call to pray for the world in a variety of different ways. What matters is not exactly how one does it, when or with whom the Christian prays, but that he or she does so, understanding this work as both holy responsibility and holy privilege. In the following chapters, we will look to the shape of the baptismal covenant itself for clues as to how the church might exercise this vocation in a deeper and more comprehensive way. But first we will ask: How, indeed, does one learn this vocation? How did my students know what to do? How do others know?

CHAPTER FOUR

Intercession and Forming Disciples

Teaching Them to Pray

How did my students learn how to pray for me so effectively? There is, of course, no simple answer to that question.

They learned some of it from what I taught them. I had emphasized using baptismal names when addressing people within the church's rites. In a class lecture on occasional services, I had taught them that emerging pastoral need sometimes calls a community to develop liturgies that address circumstances not covered in the church's authorized service books. In those situations, the faithful do best when they dialogue with what they already know, and especially the deep wisdom of the church's tradition. I had lectured on that concept, but there can be a gap between hearing a theory and applying it well. In any event, I had taught my students some things, and thus will accept some of the credit. In turn, however, I must credit my doctoral mentor, Horace T. Allen Jr., who influenced much of my thinking and teaching on pastoral rites. In a sense, when Professor Allen taught me in the early 1990s he was also teaching my students how to pray for me in November of 2010, and so on. Nevertheless, the classroom is not the only place where spiritual formation occurs—far from it.

Much of what my students had learned about praying for me came from living within the community of faith, and that living had occurred at our school, in their churches, and in communities of faith that they had known long before they showed up in our halls. Christian lives take shape as we associate with Jesus and his friends, doing what those friends usually do—caring for those in distress, defending the weak, and giving thanks for every good gift; not to mention singing hymns and songs, listening to scripture, breaking bread together, and interceding for the world. In the midst of such practices, Christians are learning how to pray. I have called this formational dynamic "holy hanging around,"[1] and it occurs, formally and informally, in all Christian communities.

Methodist tradition has embodied such a dynamic in the class-meeting pattern, which some contemporary United Methodists have been trying to revive for the contemporary church.[2] The class-meeting practice began in 1739 when some persons whose faith had been awakened by John Wesley's preaching came to him asking for advice on "how to flee from the wrath to come." He charged them to meet together weekly under the guidance of class leaders, laypersons who would organize their reflections around three foci known as the General Rules. Persons were to give evidence of their desire for conversion by (1) "doing no harm"; (2) "by doing good"; and (3) "by attending upon all the ordinances of God"—specifically public worship, prayer, scripture study, fasting, and Holy Communion.[3] Wesley's treatise on the General Rules does not mention baptism, primarily because—given the English state church system—most (if not all) of those who came to him had already been baptized. Nevertheless, many of the baptized had not been deeply formed in the faith. If we understand Christian initiation as not only the baptismal rite but also the formational processes that precede and follow it, then the dynamic of the General Rules is unmistakably initiatory. It calls people toward an ever-deepening conversion.

A similar process has been at work in ancient and contemporary catechumenal systems. As you will recall from chapter 2, the catechumenate has been a process whereby Christians have prepared for baptism and subsequent participation in both the Eucharist and the prayer of the church. They have done so through hearing the gospel and through engaging in its practices under the guidance of their sponsors and catechists. Notice the sequence: before they join the church to intercede for others by offering the prayers of their lips, those who seek baptism join the church in active mission work, interceding for those in need through the works of their hands and feet. According to the witness of the gospel, one can expect to meet the risen Christ in the midst of such embodied ministries of compassion and justice (Matt. 25:31-46), just as we expect to meet him in the midst of the liturgical assembly (Luke 24:13-35). We will investigate these catechumenal models and ask what they suggest about forming Christians for the baptismal vocation to prayer.

Meeting Christ in the World: The Catechumenate, Ancient and Contemporary, and Its Emphasis on Behavior

We return to a text that we first encountered in the second chapter, *The Apostolic Tradition* (*AT*), examining its description of the entrance into the catechumenate. As we noted before, *AT* reflects practices that may date to as early as the beginning of the third century. Notice that one did not arrive at the entry point by oneself, but rather one came with witnesses. The testimony of these witnesses was sought not on what the prospective candidate believed (or did not believe), but rather on his or her behavior. Hear this passage from the section addressing activities, crafts and professions:

> If one is a whore master he should stop or be excluded.
>
> If one is a maker of idols or a painter, he should learn that he should not make idols; and if he is not convinced that he should stop, he should be excluded. If one attends the circus, he should stop or be excluded.
>
> He who attends pagan festivals should stop or be excluded.
>
> One who is a gladiator or teaches gladiators or swordsmanship or military skills or weapons training should stop or be excluded.
>
> A soldier in the sovereign's army should not kill, or if he is ordered to kill, he should refuse. If he stops, so be it; otherwise he should be excluded.[4]

These demands may sound too harsh to our contemporary ears, but in each case the church was asking a fundamental question that must not be ignored: Had the candidate begun the process of metanoia, that is, the turn toward God? Given contemporary understandings of catechesis, we may be surprised by the lack of doctrinal examination at this beginning point. Doctrinal and liturgical issues would be addressed within the process, but at a much later point. During much of the catechumenate, they would focus on hearing and doing the Word of God. In some ways, this catechumenal process followed a spirituality characteristic of the biblical prophets, many of whom were well acquainted with the liturgical rites of their day; nevertheless, they tended to suspect them, and for good reason. Too often ritual practices have been used as a cover for injustice and a substitute for mercy. In a well-known expression of this suspicion, Amos proclaimed,

> I hate, I despise your festivals, and I take no delight in your solemn assemblies. Even though you offer me your burnt offerings and grain offerings, I will not accept them; and the offerings of well-being of your fatted animals I will not look upon. Take away from me the noise of your songs; I will not listen to the melody of your harps. But let justice roll down like waters, and righteousness like an ever-flowing stream. (Amos 5:21-24)

Right practice of the liturgy cannot be separated from the treatment of one's neighbor. In that sense, the ancient catechumenal process witnessed in *AT* agreed with the prophets that one begins to learn the liturgy under the tutelage of loving service. Justice and mercy are the proper school of prayer, and according to *AT*, it could take awhile to learn it, as long as three years of hearing the word. But even here, the emphasis was placed on one's formation resulting in changed behavior, and not on completing some type of three-year curriculum; and so, "if they learn and meditate well, do not judge them for the time, but let them be judged only by their action."[5]

A Spanish pilgrim named Egeria witnessed to a similar dynamic at work in late fourth-century Jerusalem (ca. 381). She described a rite that occurred toward the end of the catechumenate, specifically the public examination of those who indicated their desire for baptism at Easter:

> On the second day of Lent . . . the bishop's chair is placed in the middle of the Great Church, the Martyrium, the presbyters sit in chairs on either side of him, and all the clergy stand. Then one by one those seeking baptism are brought up, men coming with their fathers and women with their mothers. As they come in one by one, the bishop asks their neighbors questions about them: "Is this person leading a good life? Does he respect his parents? Is he a drunkard or a boaster?" He asks about all the serious human vices. And if his inquiries show him that someone has not committed any of these misdeeds, he himself puts down his name; but if someone is guilty, he is told to go away, and the bishop tells him that he is to amend his ways before he may come to the font.[6]

While it is a mistake to expect uniformity among the various ancient accounts of prebaptismal formation, the emphasis on behavior and character formation in Egeria is strikingly similar to what one sees in *AT*. In both cases, the emphasis is expressed negatively: in *AT* against forbidden crafts and professions, and in Egeria against "the serious human vices." Each echoes the call to repentance and renunciation that was present at the first Christian baptisms (Acts 2:38; cf. Matt. 3:2) and remains in our contemporary baptismal rites, and that call emphasizes behavior. We have no way of knowing whether these enrollment disciplines were practiced as severely as the texts suggest. Remember that both *AT* and Egeria describe public rites, and the church's public rituals always witness to its aspirations as much as they do to present realities. Moreover, those who write such descriptions often stand among the church's most committed and demanding members. In spite of these caution flags that I am raising, we should take the negative trajectory seriously and learn from it. In many cases one must say a decisive "no" on the way to the "yes" that God desires, leaving behind harmful patterns on the way to practices that enhance life. Although it remains a central part of traditional Christian wisdom, groups like Alcoholics Anonymous may understand this spiritual dynamic better than the church.

Even if one imagines this more positive spiritual trajectory, for example, moving from violence to God's shalom, one still has to learn Christian behavior and compassion. Although the Holy Spirit assists this formation process, within the context of the church, it does not occur naturally. The Roman Catholic *Rite of Christian Initiation of Adults* (*RCIA*), the leading contemporary version of the catechumenate, presents this more positive formational dynamic. One enters the period of the catechumenate, coming into a circle of caring and formation embodied in the life and witness "of sponsors, godparents, and the entire Christian community."[7] Priests, catechists, and especially sponsors help persons learn what embodied Christian faith looks like, and they help shape religious behavior and attitudes. According to the *RCIA*, catechumens learn the shape of Christ's love by seeing it practiced and by participating in it:

> Thus formed (by the Word of God), "the newly converted set out on a spiritual journey. Already sharing through faith in the mystery of Christ's death and resurrection, they pass from the old to a new nature made perfect in Christ. Since this transition brings with it a progressive change of outlook and conduct, it should become manifest by means of its social consequences and it should develop gradually during the period of the catechumenate."[8]

Along the way, persons are learning to pray. As they serve others and engage in conversation with them, they learn to notice their needs in a deeper and more comprehensive way, and thus an intercessory imagination begins to take shape within them. Such formation takes time as one is progressively drawn beyond one's own preoccupations and toward a wider vision of life in God. Echoing the patience witnessed in *AT*, the *RCIA* insists that one cannot put a strict timetable on such formation:

> The time spent in the catechumenate should be long enough—several years if necessary—for the conversion and faith of the catechumen to

> become strong. By their formation in the entire Christian life and sufficiently prolonged probation the catechumens are properly initiated into the mysteries of salvation and the practice of an evangelical way of life.[9]

Again, the ancient precedent of the catechumenal ordo suggests that one learn to make intercession through exercising one's hands and feet before one learns to intercede using the voice. The rubrics of the *RCIA* follow this logic that we saw earlier in Justin Martyr and *AT* (chapter 2), as one takes part in the general intercessions for the first time only after baptism.[10] I do not wish to emphasize a strict reading of this paragraph in the *RCIA*. Rather, as before, I wish to emphasize the vocation that the baptized must fulfill rather than prohibitions directed toward those who have not yet been baptized. Indeed, such prohibitions may not be pastorally feasible in many contexts such as my own United Methodism, which (for better or worse) has tended to allow seekers to participate in the full range of the church's liturgical life, not only allowing Communion to be offered to the nonbaptized, but also defending it. For United Methodists, restricting participation in the prayers of the people might seem doubly absurd. Nevertheless, the catechumenal ordo has much to teach us about formation for intercessory work—it should include active engagement in mission, especially with and for persons in poverty; and it should also include engagement with wounded creation. Such formation could work in concert with teaching new Christians how to use the prayer forms of the church and how to formulate extemporaneous prayers. At the least, one does mission and one learns to pray at the same time, and one continues to learn the praxis of intercession in the same way, through active *diakonia*, that is, through service. As Jesus said to his disciples, "Whoever wishes to become great among you must be your servant [*diákonos*] . . . for the Son of Man came not to be served but to serve [*diakonéo*]" (Mark 10:43, 45). In this sense, the catechumenate is not another program from which one graduates, but it is a sign to the church, calling everyone in the church to continuing formation. As such, it raises an important question about intercessory work: Where does liturgy end and mission begin? It is best when the distinctions are not easily made, when the two keep flowing in and out of each other—one continuous stream of living water.

Diakonia and Continued Formation for the Work of Intercession

As we see in the previous paragraph, this Greek word *diakonia* appears in the New Testament in both noun and verb forms, a dynamic that is reflected in the English words *service* and *servant*. Our word *deacon* is a more direct borrowing from the Greek word, and, indeed, the church's work of servant ministry is given particular embodiment in the work of ordained deacons.[11] As the work of the catechumenate is an example to the church, teaching them to pray, so is the work of the deacon, as long as it does not become a substitute for the work of the whole church. Traditionally, deacons have stood at the door of the church, sometimes guarding those doors as witnessed in this text from *The Didascalia of the Apostles*:

> As regards the deacons, let one of them stand continually near the offerings of the Eucharist, and let another stand outside near the door and pay attention to those who enter. . . . If anyone finds himself in a place not his own, let the deacon who is inside take him, make him get up, and lead him to his proper place.[12]

In a better sense, deacons lead the baptized faithful out from the assembly, past the threshold where the font often stands, into their mission of caring for their community and world. The church then asks those deacons to gather a list of the various needs encountered in that mission, bringing them back through the church doors to be offered at the next gathering of the congregation. As one keeps this diaconal rhythm, the ability to see those needs in a wider and more comprehensive manner increases over time.

We see an example of deacons leading such prayers in Egeria. As she describes it, during Lucernare (i.e., Evening Prayer/Vespers), the deacon would read "the normal commemoration of individuals," and then others would sing the *kyrie eleison* ("Lord, have mercy") response.[13] The practice of the deacon leading prayers has been particularly well maintained within Eastern Orthodoxy, and with the revival of the permanent diaconate in the Western churches, we have opportunity to restore this practice.[14] Again, such work is both liturgy and mission.

Like the Roman Catholic Church, United Methodism has only recently emphasized the development of a permanent diaconate. Prior to more recent developments, ordination as deacon had been a relatively brief transitional step on the way to ordination as a presbyter (i.e., priest or elder).[15] For instance, in John Wesley's *Sunday Service for the Methodists in America*, the prayer for the ordination of a deacon refers to an inferior office that one hopes to shed on the way to a more significant ecclesiastical office, perhaps like a sixteen-year-old hopes to leave behind his junior driver's license upon reaching his eighteenth birthday:

> Almighty God, giver of all good things, who of thy great goodness hast vouchsafed to accept and take these thy servants into the office of deacons in thy church; make them, we beseech thee, O Lord, to be modest, humble, and constant in their ministration, and to have a ready will to observe all spiritual discipline; that they always having the testimony of a good conscience, and continuing ever stable and strong in thy Son Christ, may so well behave themselves in this inferior office, that they may be found worthy to be called unto the higher ministries in thy church, through the same thy Son our Savior Jesus Christ to whom be glory and honor world without end. *Amen.*[16]

For Catholics, the development of a permanent deacon has occurred since Vatican II and *Lumen Gentium*.[17] For United Methodists the change came even later, with the vote of the 1996 General Conference.[18] In many ways Methodists remain in a transitional state in which we struggle with some significant confusions. On the one hand, pastors who were formed under the previous praxis may experience significant difficulty viewing deacons as other than junior colleagues, only now they have no possibility of shedding their inferior status. On the other hand, the fact that we formerly allowed all of our deacons to preside at the Eucharist in parishes where they served as pastors has led some to seek so-called sacramental privileges for the current version of the diaconal office.[19] The argument presents theological problems on a variety of fronts, the first being that all of the baptized have sacramental privileges (and responsibilities!), albeit varying and complementary ones; that is, after all, a major thesis of baptismal ecclesiology. A second problem, which relates to the first, is that when deacons call for the elders to share an occasional small morsel of their presidential privilege, they unwittingly reinforce the view that elders do the really important work during the Eucharist, while the rest of the church essentially watches them do it. Why is the deacon's preparing of the altar not as significant as the presbyter's proclamation of the Great Thanksgiving, or for that matter, a steward's baking of the bread and the congregation's "Amen"? The whole church does the eucharistic work, and each part is incomplete without the other.

Given this baptismal ecclesiology, deacons would do a greater service to the church were they to focus on their traditional liturgical role, particularly that of leading the intercessions of the assembly. In doing so, deacons could help the entire church pray better and more deeply. Given the impoverished state of public intercessions within The United Methodist Church, that would be a significant contribution for its deacons to make. Unfortunately, since deacons are not subject to the bishop's appointment, in the majority of cases only more affluent churches have been able to afford them.[20] In the absence of a deacon, however, others could be formed to do this work for the church, for diakonia does not belong to deacons alone, and the spirit of service is at the heart of all intercessory work.

As it is with catechumens, so it continues following baptism—embodied service continues to form us for prayer. As such, churches should provide ample opportunities for local and short-term mission work. Some will argue that such efforts do little good, and may in fact be counterproductive, because they do not adequately address the root causes of poverty. They may even mask them, quieting the consciences of those complicit in that poverty. It can be a legitimate complaint, especially when one considers the growing phenomenon of youth mission trips that look suspiciously like vacations. Every time I hear this critique, however, I remember my friend

Michael Kirwan (d. 1999), who committed his life to the Catholic Worker movement, directing the Lewellyn Scott House of Hospitality on T. Street in Washington, D.C., and its sister property, the John Filiger Farm near Alderson, West Virginia. Mike knew that church work groups—such as our Methodists from Chambersburg, Pennsylvania—often came to the house or the farm out of a naive desire to do something good, perhaps the proverbial service to "those less fortunate." We did projects in both places, at the house in the summer of 1987 and at the farm in 1988, for motives not unlike those held by others. Michael was happy when such persons would come, and received them as generously as his homeless guests. Why so? He claimed that the Catholic Worker functioned like a "school of compassion" for such church visitors, and in this and in any school, we know that the lessons affect some more deeply than others.

I was deeply affected by the experience, although I can't say exactly what happened to me or why it occurred. I know that my decision to risk giving up my parish appointment in order to prepare myself as a liturgical scholar was influenced by Mike's boldness, and also by the combination of justice and prayer that stands at the heart of the Catholic Worker movement. I've never been able to get the Catholic Worker witness out of my heart and mind, and others from our group carry its effects within them as well.

Again, many will argue that work camps and service projects do not address the causes of poverty and injustice. Fair enough, and we could raise a similar critique about praying in general. In many cases prayer works healing more than it works a cure. Sometimes it does both, and sometimes we can see little of either. If we don't see a direct result, should we stop praying? In a similar manner, what if people are changed by the work camp experience or by doing relatively unnoticed works of mercy? Nevertheless, one changed perspective can impact many others, and so any changed perspective becomes potentially profound.[21] There is no insignificant positive or negative action. We are told that a butterfly that moves its wings at the equator can affect air currents hundreds of miles away,[22] and we know that a woman who refuses an order to move to the back of the bus in Birmingham can help topple Jim Crow throughout an entire nation. So does prayer change things? The answer is both yes and no. Does charity work change society? The answer is both yes and no, and perhaps only God needs to know exactly how it does so.

In a conversation that followed a presentation I made on formation for prayer, a priest shared with me about youth in his church who served breakfast once a week at a ministry for homeless persons. During the prayers that they offered as part of their weekly youth meetings, these young persons began praying for those they had served, and they were praying for them by name.[23] Serving in a food ministry was teaching them to pray. Speaking these names in prayer could seem a relatively small thing, and it will not quickly end the problems of homelessness and hunger. By naming them, however, these youth were beginning to carry them in their hearts. When we consider persons our friends, it is much harder to ignore their struggles.

In the next section of this chapter, we will return to St. Gregory of Nyssa Episcopal Church in San Francisco to look at a context where the missional and intercessory dynamic works in a profound way.

Praying with St. Gregory of Nyssa: A Profound Example of Diakonia

Sara Miles, Director of Ministry at St. Gregory's, makes the bold claim, "Every single thing the resurrected Jesus does on earth he does through our bodies."[24] She told me, "We're to become Jesus." I listened to her carefully and checked my understanding—she did not merely say "like Jesus."[25] While boldly put, it is no bolder than the language of Paul, who told the first-century Christians in Corinth, "You are the body of Christ and individually members of it" (1 Cor. 12:27). We intercede with Christ, and he intercedes for the world in and through us. Again, when the church sends its catechumens into the world to learn how to serve, it is teaching them to pray. Such embodiment is the foundation for the spoken petitions that come later. The fact that I am citing St. Gregory's to illustrate a spiritual dynamic that I identify within the catechumenate is somewhat ironic, given that they have no catechumenate and do not intend to begin one. According to their rector, Paul Fromberg, a restored catechumenate could become "a form of bullying," and he went on to express skepticism as to whether such an ancient pattern can make sense when dropped into a contemporary context.[26] As to the bullying remark, he was referring to St. Gregory's well-documented core commitment to communing the nonbaptized, which (as we have seen) is the polar opposite to the praxis of the catechumenal way. If, then, we look only to the link between baptism and Communion and the controversies surrounding that discussion,[27] then St. Gregory's is by no means a catechumenal place. But if we can look past that fact for a while, then we see that it is an assembly that is learning how to pray through their bodies, and in that way it has much in common with the missional dynamic of the catechumenate as I described it earlier. Said Fromberg, "What matters is what you do,"[28] and the faith of the church is shown not so much in the words of its creeds, but in what the church does.

Nowhere is this dynamic seen more clearly than in the work of The Food Pantry that takes place at St. Gregory's, especially when one views it in relation to the church's liturgies. According to Miles, "The Pantry presents everything in the church that drives you crazy and everything that is beautiful about the church." It is a place of healing, she insists, because it is modeled on the sacraments and not on a social service program. Many of those who come for food are also participants in the work.[29] It is not run by the rules of the world, where the strongest rule, but rather "it is done to praise God and to join in God's work. It is done to raise the dead."[30]

The best understanding of the connection between the liturgies of the Eucharist at St. Gregory's and The Food Pantry begins in their eucharistic space. There is no chancel rail to separate clergy and choir from the rest of the faithful, but rather a rotunda with an elegant hardwood floor, with an altar standing at the center of it all. It is primarily a space for the gathering of the assembly, and in some ways it is a dance floor. When it is time for the Eucharist, priests, lay liturgical leaders, choir members, and the rest of the assembly move to the altar and stand around it in concentric circles. Above the congregation, on the walls of the rotunda, are icons of the dancing saints depicted in mid-step, moving counterclockwise around the altar,[31] as if drawn into the eternal dance of the Holy Trinity. After the congregation receives Communion, the whole assembly joins in a circle dance that moves in the same counterclockwise direction suggested by the icons. As the cantor calls out the steps, one places a hand on the shoulder of the person directly to the front, and then one takes a step to the right. Then the left foot crosses the right, followed by a second step with the right. Then one lifts the left knee and moves it toward the right, and then lifts the right knee and moves it to the left. It's a bit complex, but no one is left out, and the learning comes in the midst of the dance. Indeed, on the Sunday I visited, I timed my arrival for the beginning of Sunday school but arrived earlier, just as the dance was commencing toward the end of the 8:30 a.m. service. Miles, having noticed me standing outside, invited me to move through the doors and join them. I stumbled my way through it that first time, but then I did much better on my second attempt, at the end of the 10:45 service. I would see this counterclockwise movement again during the following Friday's Food Pantry.

The Food Pantry day begins like every other weekday at St. Gregory's, with Morning Prayer at eight o'clock. That daily service includes psalmody, readings, and prayers for others, followed by a procession to the font, which is located outside the door of the rotunda (see chapter 2). The dismissal occurs at the font as the leader says,

> Almighty God, you have brought us through the night
> and led us to your living water;
> Now mark us as your own as we take your love into the world;
> There is no Jew or Greek, slave or free, male or female anymore:
> Make us all one in Jesus Christ.[32]

Water is placed on each person's forehead, and all respond with the "Amen." This daily dismissal underscores the missional trajectory of the font, as persons are sent forth to continue the work of thanksgiving and the intercession that they have offered. On Food Pantry days that intention is expressed in an even more emphatic manner, with a connection that has been present since the beginning of this ministry. Indeed, Miles launched The Food Pantry in 2000, on the same weekend that she was baptized at St. Gregory's.[33] Soon after Morning Prayer, trucks loaded with fresh fruit and vegetables begin arriving at the loading area, which is located in the same area as the baptismal font. So their baptismal space is also a workspace, the one flowing into the other.

In like manner, the eucharistic space—including the altar—becomes a staging area for the food distribution. They take precautions, and so they cover their hardwood floors with pads; the altar is covered with a tablecloth and holds snacks and supplies during the pantry service. Isabel directed the process, while Miles and Fromberg went to the kitchen to make lunch. As the trucks arrived from the San Francisco food bank, we brought in all manner of fresh produce—cabbage, celery, cantaloupe, strawberries, and tomatoes. All of these were placed at stations surrounding the altar.

Conversations sprang up as the preparatory work progressed. I fell into conversation with a retired chef who was making his second visit to the pantry. He said, "It's always fresh here, never any of the rejects." As I would see, it matters. After the volunteers finished the staging work and took a coffee break, Isabel said to us, "Now it is time for groceries." The point here, as Miles said, is that many of those who volunteer also come because they need the food. For them, The Food Pantry at St. Gregory's gives not only food but also the dignity of working and serving. It was wonderful talking with the old chef, who was something of a food philosopher. He said that every meal should be "a circus of the mouth. . . . If it doesn't taste great," he said, "then don't serve it."

Given the context, the conversation in and around the food was fascinating. Someone that day remarked that San Francisco is "full of foodies," and St. Gregory's fits well in this milieu. Their love of food flows in and out of their sacramental-missional praxis. Indeed, Fromberg loves to cook, and his primary Friday task is preparing lunch for the volunteers. On the day I was there he made wild boar stew. When one person heard the menu for the day, she thought he was kidding, but no, one of the volunteers had shot a boar and donated it to the pantry; and the stew was particularly good, drawing the "circus of the mouth" comment. Right before lunch was served at 11:30 a.m., tables were set up around the food that we had already set out for the pantry, and places were set. So the lunch tables were the outside of two concentric circles surrounding the altar, with the food to be distributed on the inside circle. One should think of this arrangement in relation to their circle dance around the same altar at the Sunday liturgy. In each case, the saints surround the altar. The lunch tables were taken down before persons began arriving at 12:30 p.m. to receive their food, but these guests also circled the altar, moving to the various stations in a counterclockwise manner. Here one sees ritual embodiment of Miles's claim that The Food Pantry is an extension of the Eucharist.[34] In some ways, it is the same thing.

Isabel assigned me to the cabbage station, with instructions to give one to each person. As I was distributing them, I began to sense the eucharistic dynamics of the process, and so I began to hold them up to the recipients, as I might present the host to a communicant. As much as I could, I tried to make eye contact and have a short exchange with each. Given the space and its resonances, it seemed right to think of what I was doing along the lines of a procession to receive the sacrament. Embodied prayer and spoken prayer were uniting in one stream. As we involve people in such embodied work, we teach them to pray, and the same work continues forming us for prayer. Such work is prayer.

We will conclude this chapter by taking a journey back to the baptismal rite of fourth-century Milan, which contains an intriguing reference to a footwashing ritual. There we find formation for prayer occurring not prior to baptism, as we have seen in the catechumenate, nor following it in continued diakonia, but as embodied prayer in the midst of the baptismal rite itself. What can footwashing teach us about formation for prayer?

Baptism and Footwashing: "We, Too, Are Not without Discernment"

We have report of the late fourth-century Milanese baptismal ordo through the mystagogical teaching of their bishop, Ambrose of Milan. Mystagogical teaching (mystagogy) refers to teaching on the sacraments, that is, on the holy mysteries. This instruction was offered to the newly baptized in the days following their baptism, and was designed to help them understand what had happened to them; as such, it also helped them comprehend the shape of their subsequent discipleship.[35] Ambrose began his teaching with a fairly conventional description of baptism and its meaning: "Yesterday we discoursed on the font . . . into which, believing in the Father and the Son and the Holy Ghost, we are received and plunged."[36]

A bit further on, Ambrose took the discussion in a different and apparently surprising direction:

> Thou camest up out of the font. What followed? The high priest . . . was girt up and washed thy feet. What is this sacrament? Doubtless thou hast heard that when the Lord had washed the feet of the other disciples, *He cometh to Peter; and Peter saith to him, Dost thou wash my feet?*[37]

We should not impose later controversies about the number of sacraments upon our reading of this late fourth-century document. Nevertheless, Ambrose defended footwashing as part of their initiatory rite. He wrote,

> We are not ignorant that the Roman Church has not this custom. Her type and form we follow in all things; however she has not this custom of washing the feet. . . . There are, however, some who say and try to urge that this ought to be done, not as a sacrament, not at baptism, not at regeneration; but only as we should wash the feet of a guest. The latter is an act of humility, the former a work of sanctification. Accordingly, learn how it is a sacrament and a means of sanctification. *Unless I wash thy feet, thou wilt have no part of me.* This I say, not to find fault with others, but to recommend my own usage. In all things I desire to follow the Roman Church. Yet we too are not without discernment.[38]

As with many ancient ritual texts, this one does not answer all of the questions that we might like to ask. At the least, however, we know that footwashing was part of the baptismal rite in Milan and that Ambrose defends it, asserting ancient precedent. More broadly, he asserts that Christians may abide in the one Spirit and yet come to differing ritual conclusions.

Whatever we make of Ambrose's witness on footwashing, in one sense he lost the argument and it did not ultimately become part of the wider church's baptism rite.[39] On the other hand, many Anabaptist churches retain it as a central piece of their ritual life, practicing it whenever the Lord's Supper is observed.[40] Thus for them it functions something like a renewal of the baptismal covenant, and in some cases is preceded by several weeks of preparation.[41] Furthermore, although footwashing is not a part of the baptismal services practiced in most Catholic and mainline Protestant churches, for many of us the witness to footwashing retains a central place, since it is the gospel for Holy Thursday evening (John 13: 1-17, 31b-35) in all three years of the lectionary cycle. In that text, Jesus addresses the church in the words quoted by Ambrose:

> Unless I wash you, you have no share with me. (John 13:8)
>
> So if I, your Lord and Teacher, have washed your feet, you also ought to wash one another's feet. For I have set you an example, that you also should do as I have done to you. (John 13:14-15)

As to the relationship between footwashing rituals and initiation, we may also take the counsel of those who suggest that we view the Triduum—the Holy Thursday, Good Friday, and Easter Vigil observances that stand at the heart of the Christian Year—as one continuous service.[42] Since the Triduum culminates with the baptismal rite of the Easter Vigil, everything in those three days points toward baptism and its meaning. The focus of those three days witnesses not only to what Jesus did on our behalf, but also to the shape of the discipleship into which we are baptized. Thus, when we see Jesus washing the feet of the disciples, we should imagine not just James, John, and the reluctant Peter receiving this particular blessing, but ourselves as well, along with the charge to wash the feet of others. Given this expanded understanding of the church's initiatory practices, footwashing remains at the heart of the church's baptismal ritual, where Ambrose insisted it should stand.

Wherever we place footwashing within the ritual life of our churches—whether within the Triduum or not—we do well to retain it, and as a practice for the entire assembly. Indeed, *The United Methodist Book of Worship* lists footwashing as an option for Holy Thursday, and provides some limited rubrics for doing it, including hymn suggestions.[43] The Presbyterian *Book of*

Common Worship and *Evangelical Lutheran Worship* also list footwashing as an option for Holy Thursday along with similar limited rubrics.[44] A rubric in *The Book of Common Prayer* Maundy Thursday rite mentions "the ceremony of the washing of feet," placing it after the Gospel and homily, but gives no further instruction as to how to proceed.[45] If we have forgotten how to do it, however, our Anabaptist sisters and brothers can teach us the finer points of its congregational practice. The most important thing, however, is to begin doing it. As with most of our ritual practice, it will remain a work in progress, and since ritual exists on a human scale, good liturgists will tolerate a little messiness, including some water sloshing over the edge of the bowl. One can always cover the floor.

But again, we should make a beginning, and if we have already done that, then we should continue. Why so? Experience convinces me that some important spiritual insights emerge only when one kneels down and washes feet. As we have seen, this spiritual dynamic extends to other forms of embodied service. There is spiritual insight and Christian formation that one cannot gain other than by feeding the poor, by visiting the sick and those in prison, not to mention changing diapers, and, I might imagine, by breast-feeding a baby. Much of what we learn we must learn first in our bodies. Although we have sometimes covered the sacraments and sacramental action with many words and theories about those words, at root the sacraments are actions and the handling of holy things.[46] The sacraments teach us what to do with our bodies in relation to other bodies and the whole creation, and this formation takes a lifetime.

So then, in this chapter we have seen that Christians learn to pray according to the wisdom of the catechumenate, that is, first in the body, through works of mercy and compassion. Nevertheless, the baptism that occurs at the conclusion of the catechumenate does not end this formative dynamic, but rather it deepens and intensifies it. As we have seen, through diakonia the embodied intercession of our hands and feet continues to shape our spoken intercessions. We notice more, and we pray. We pray more, and we notice. As we will see in the next chapter, baptism further intensifies our vocation by sending us to the foot of the cross. Our intercessory work continues there, both in our bodies and in the words that we eventually try to speak.

CHAPTER FIVE

Intercession and The Baptismal Covenant

Standing Beneath the Cross with the Faithful

In baptism, we participate in the dying and rising of Christ; we enter what some theologians call the "Paschal Mystery." As we noted in the previous chapter, the story that we hear on Holy Thursday, Good Friday, and Easter is no longer merely a story about what happened to Jesus. It becomes our story, the shape God intends for our discipleship. One finds reminders of this spiritual dynamic all over the New Testament. As we have seen, Jesus insisted that his followers join him in washing feet (John 13:14-15). He told his disciples, "If any want to become my followers, let them deny themselves and take up their cross and follow me" (Mark 8:34). Looking toward his crucifixion, he asked James and John, "Are you able to drink the cup that I drink, or be baptized with the baptism that I am baptized with?" (Mark 10:38). They would do so, he told them, and by extension so do we. The reference to baptism is unavoidable. Do not overlook the fact that the evangelist who told this story was part of a church that had been baptizing for more than three decades, and thus it appears that he saw the connection between baptism and the call to participate in Christ's suffering.

In the sixth chapter of Romans, Paul brings the matter to greater clarity:

> Do you not know that all of us who have been baptized into Christ Jesus were baptized into his death? Therefore we have been buried with him by baptism into death, so that, just as Christ was raised from the dead by the glory of the Father, so we too might walk in newness of life. (vv. 3-4)

Paul's baptismal theology asserts what God has already done, but it does not end there. He points to what God is doing in us now, through that same baptism:

> So you also must consider yourselves dead to sin and alive to God in Christ Jesus. . . . No longer present your members to sin as instruments of wickedness, but present yourselves to God as those who have been brought from death to life, and present your members to God as instruments of righteousness. (vv. 11, 13)

Once again—the baptized are called to participate in God's mission, presenting our members (that is, our bodies) to God as instruments (or weapons)[1] of righteousness. If we use this variant translation, "weapons," we must understand that this is yet another instance of New Testament writers taking a common term and breaking it toward a new meaning shaped by Christ.[2] That is, just as Jesus the King reigns not from an ornate throne room, but from the cross (Luke 23:32-43), so these "weapons" are not swords or spears, but acts of compassion and love such as our intercessions.

Holding with Paul's metaphor of dying with Christ, we offer our prayers in the midst of death, that is, while standing at the foot of the cross. But how do we do that today, given that the events on Golgotha happened nearly two thousand years ago? We find important clues in classic Good Friday practices deeply rooted in scripture. From those, we may find our way to the foot of the cross, even as we encounter it in our own neighborhoods. As with Maundy Thursday and the washing of the feet, Good Friday is about what happened to Jesus, but it is also points to the shape of our discipleship.

Good Friday and Its Classic Intercessory Agenda

We begin our discussion of Good Friday by returning to fourth-century Jerusalem, where Holy Week practices began. Although the Great Vigil of Easter developed as early as the second century,[3] discrete Maundy Thursday and Good Friday observances did not emerge until the fourth century. These began to spread throughout the Christian world as pilgrims to the Holy City experienced them and then adapted them for use in other places. Our friend Egeria was one such pilgrim. She offered a description of the Good Friday afternoon service in Jerusalem, sometime around 381 CE:

> At midday they go before the Cross. . . . The whole time between midday and three o'clock is taken up with readings. They are all about the things that Jesus suffered: first the psalms on this subject, then the Apostles (the Epistles or Acts) which concern it, then passages from the Gospels . . . and between all the readings are prayers, all of them appropriate to the day.[4]

Notice the emphasis on the reading of Scripture. Although they read from many passages, the reference to suffering suggests that they also read from the Passion narratives, those long accounts of the events surrounding Christ's death (Matt. 26:1–27:66; Mark 14:1–15:47; Luke 22:1–23:56; John 18:1–19:42). In these, they heard of his physical suffering—the scourging, the nails in his hands and feet, and his thirst—but not only that. The Passion narratives speak to the pain of his loneliness and abandonment by friends, and his pain as the crowd turned against him, shouting "Crucify him!" He suffered Judas' betrayal as well as Peter's denial. He suffered false accusation and an unjust legal process. There was the pain of ridicule: "Hail, King of the Jews!" Jesus suffered public humiliation, even of a sexual nature—likely he was crucified in the nude[5]—along with the feeling that God had abandoned him altogether. His suffering encompassed much of what human beings have suffered then and now, and the people who heard these accounts along with Egeria responded emotionally. But their participation did not end there. Note Egeria's reference to the "appropriate" prayers that they offered in response to the readings. We might like to ask her, "So then, sister, what appropriate prayers did they offer? Tell us more," but she does not answer that question. We can speculate, however, and not without some foundation.

A set of prayers known as the Good Friday intercessions have existed at least since the fourth century, and some scholars date them as early as the third. They are "the oldest form of the prayer of the faithful in the Roman Rite."[6] Nine categories were covered: "for the church, for the pope, for all ranks of the people of God, for the emperor, for catechumens, for those with various needs, for heretics and schismatics, for Jews, and for pagans."[7] One category at a time, the priest would bid the assembly to pray. Silence would ensue, perhaps with persons kneeling, followed by a collect, and then the corporate amen.[8] While preserved within the fourth-century text mentioned here, likely these petitions existed well before that, and were used not only at Good Friday but at other times as well.[9] That scholars have found them within ancient Good Friday rites can be read as evidence of a tendency that Anton Baumstark named the Second Law of Liturgical Evolution," specifically that "primitive conditions are maintained with greater tenacity in the most sacred seasons of the Liturgical Year."[10] So again, these petitions may be much older than the fourth century.

Regardless of their precise origins and ancient usage, the tradition of the Good Friday intercessions has been maintained and the church continues to shape it. The contemporary practice is supported by the biblical texts for Good Friday as appointed within the Revised Common Lectionary, particularly Hebrews 10:16-25 and the Johannine Passion narrative, John 18:1–19:42. The Hebrews text presents Jesus as "a great high priest over the house of God" and then exhorts the faithful, "Let us approach with a true heart in full assurance of faith" (Heb. 10:21-22). We do our priestly work of intercession along with him. The narrative in John's Gospel portrays that priest at work, as it were, presiding over his own sacrifice. When Pilate confronts him and claims to have power to release him, Jesus responds, "You would have no power over me unless it had been given you from above" (John 19:10-11). In John, Jesus carries the cross "by himself" (John 19:17). No help is needed (compare Matt. 27:32; Mark 15:21; Luke 23:26). When Jesus dies, he does so willingly and only after all of his work has been finished—he "bowed his head and gave up his spirit "(John 19:28-30). In no way does the Johannine Passion deny the suffering of Jesus and its horrors (see John 18:12; 19:1-3, 15-18, 34, 38-42); but clearly it presents Jesus as the one in charge of the events, again, a priest presiding over his own sacrifice.[11] Moreover, we have a place in this narrative, as we will see. So again, the Good Friday readings proclaim the Great High Priest Jesus at his work, and they call us to participate in his intercessory work.

The Book of Common Prayer (1979) Good Friday liturgy exhorts the assembly to join the prayers:

> Dear People of God: Our heavenly Father sent his Son into the world not to condemn the world, but that the world through him might be saved; that all who believe in him might be delivered from the power of sin and death, and become heirs with him of everlasting life.
>
> We pray, therefore, for people everywhere according to their needs.[12]

Then follows the solemn collects, a long series of prayers patterned on the ancient biddings structure noted above: bidding, silence, collect, corporate amen. Prayers are offered for "the holy Church of Christ throughout the world," for Christians in the community and those to be baptized. Prayers are offered for "all nations and peoples of the earth, and for those in authority," including the courts, and "for all who suffer, and are afflicted in body or in mind." Finally, prayers are offered "for all those who have not received the Gospel of Christ," including "those who in the name of Christ have persecuted others." It is a wide and comprehensive prayer agenda. The text for these prayers covers three pages, and given the period of silence after each series of biddings, moving through them should take a significant amount of time.[13] These intercessions constitute the primary corporate work of the Good Friday liturgy. Similar Good Friday prayers are provided in the Presbyterian *Book of Common Worship*[14] and, of course, in the Roman Catholic rite.[15] *Evangelical Lutheran* Worship provides a list of the biddings, although no further texts are offered in support of them.[16] While *The United Methodist Book of Worship* appoints the same lectionary readings as these other churches, there is no reference to the classic Good Friday prayer structure, only a call for "Concerns and Prayers," with no guidance given as to their content or purpose. The Good Friday reproaches, "Christ's Lament against His Faithless Church," provide a long prayer of confession that suggests an intercessory agenda—for instance, "I was hungry, but you gave me no food, thirsty, but you gave me no drink"[17]—but it goes unfulfilled. One is left with the sense that the purpose of Good Friday is to feel sorrow, which may be an appropriate response. Nevertheless, it is incomplete. Addressing this divergence from ecumenical Good Friday practice could significantly improve intercessory practice within United Methodism.

This tradition of the Good Friday intercessions calls us to exercise our baptismal priesthood, and also speaks to its ongoing shape. What is that shape? As we pray, we attend to the suffering of Jesus. In a sense, we stand at the foot of the cross, interceding for those who suffer. To arrive at a better understanding of such praying, we look to a particular scene in John's Passion narrative, along with some iconography and hymnody that reflect upon it. As we've been doing, we'll also look to more scripture and other historical Christian sources. Then we will move back to contemporary narrative.

Interceding for Those Who Suffer: Standing Beneath the Cross with the Faithful

As we have already noted, in John's Passion narrative, we see Christ as a priest presiding over his own sacrifice, and we have a place in that narrative. Where is it? Many have perceived an invitation to discipleship in this scene:

> Meanwhile, standing near the cross of Jesus were his mother, and his mother's sister, Mary the wife of Clopas, and Mary Magdalene. When Jesus saw his mother and the disciple whom he loved standing beside her, he said to his mother, "Woman, here is your son." Then he said to

> the disciple, "Here is your mother." And from that hour the disciple took her into his own home. (John 19:25-27)

Notice that they are standing near the cross. Whereas the synoptic narratives place others in and around the cross—religious leaders and passersby deriding Jesus (Matt. 27:39; Mark 15:29-32); soldiers mocking him (Luke 23:36-37); and bandits (or a bandit) taunting him (Matt. 27:44; Luke 23:39; compare Mark 15:27), in those narratives the disciples have fled. Some of the women who "had followed [him] from Galilee" were watching the scene, but only "from a distance" (Matt. 27:55; Mark 15:40-41). One finds expressions of faith within these narratives—the thief who asked Jesus to remember him (Luke 23:40-43); and the centurion who proclaimed him "God's Son" (Mark 15:39). But according to Matthew, Mark, and Luke, those who had been his disciples did not come near, and given the imperial threat so graphically and publicly expressed in the Crucifixion, one can hardly blame them. Even the distant presence of the women is courageous.

We err, of course, if we try to construct a harmonized account of these events. Even a quick surface reading of the accounts won't allow it. Already these narratives, brought to final shape across the latter parts of the first century, bear the marks of a church hearing them through the eyes of faith. In like manner, we should hear them as windows into discipleship or, for that matter, as examples of nonfaith. Will we look at suffering and add to it by blaming the victims? Will we run away from those who suffer? Will we participate in executions, or passively allow them to continue? Or will we cry for mercy and help others find faith in the midst of suffering? We have the grace to decide. As my colleague Alyce McKenzie has said it so well, "Every year I stand here harboring the foolish hope that, this year, the outcome will be different. His choice is not going to change. But isn't there the chance that ours could."[18]

And so this scene in John's Gospel invites us to faith. We see the faithful women, the mother of Jesus, her sister, and the other two Marys standing near the suffering one. They are a microcosm of the church. They cannot extricate Jesus from that day's suffering—indeed, he chose it—but they remain on the scene nonetheless, refusing to abandon him. Sometimes standing near the suffering one is the most that one can do, but that is not always the case. In another biblical text, we hear Jesus tell his disciples, "Just as you did it to one of the least of these who are members of my family, you did it to me" (Matt. 25:40). The crucified Christ is also the rape victim, the murder victim, the battered child or spouse. Refusing to abandon them means defending them. The crucified Christ is the man on death row, perhaps unjustly condemned, like Jesus, perhaps not. He is the starving child and the homeless man without a coat. Where is the suffering Christ? Hold that question for a moment while we consider another one.

Who is this other one who shows up in John's narrative, this "disciple whom he loved" (John 19:26)? We find him at other key places throughout the fourth Gospel: beside Jesus at that last meal (John 13:23); and at the post-Resurrection breakfast by the Sea of Galilee, where Jesus called Peter and others to follow him even to the place of death (John 21:15-23). In that final scene of the Gospel, the author tells us that this "disciple whom Jesus loved" is the writer of the Gospel (John 21:20, 24), so we could simply say that he is John, only John, and be done with the question. But the phrase is more open-ended than that. Isn't each one of us "the disciple whom Jesus loved," called to hear the testimony of the gospel and believe, called to trust in God's abiding love for us and the entire world? If we allow ourselves to hear the text in this more open-ended manner, then we can imagine Jesus addressing each of us from the cross, looking at his mother and her friends, and saying to us, "Here is your mother," and by extension, "Here are her friends." "Join them in their vocation and take them under your care." And so we—disciples whom Jesus loves—join them at the foot of the cross, attending to the suffering Christ wherever we find him.

Classic Eastern Orthodox iconography of the Crucifixion may help us here. In many cases, one does not see the crucified Christ alone, but the scenes are populated by others standing beneath him: Mary and the faithful women, along with the beloved disciple.[19] The point of these icons is not to paint a realistic picture of the scene—we don't have any photographs—but to provide believers a window that allows us to go to a similar place spiritually. We become the faithful, praying with the suffering Christ. He is, of course, also our High Priest. While Protestants do not normally pray with icons,[20] their hymns work in a similar manner, inviting them to share in the spiritual dynamics of biblical scenes. Thus we sing "Beneath the cross of Jesus I fain would take my stand."[21] We sing "Were you there when they crucified my Lord?"[22] "Go to Dark Gethsemane" exhorts us to "watch with him one bitter hour" (that is, in prayer) and then "Calvary's mournful mountain climb."[23] We go to Calvary's mountain by attending to those who suffer, even seeking them out. We take their wounds seriously, refusing to abandon them. We defend them, interceding with actions as well as with our words. Such praying is realistic, but hopeful, rather like the doctor who gives a clear and detailed diagnosis about your cancer, but then lays out an equally clear therapeutic plan, even if palliative care emerges as the most compassionate option. I have come to call such intercessory work the "anti-docetic" way of prayer. It takes its place under the cross, where death is named death, evil is called evil, and suffering is never ignored; neither is it hidden under euphemisms. Neither death, nor evil, nor suffering, however, is given the last word.

I have discussed the problem of docetic spirituality in some of my earlier work,[24] although the term *anti-docetic* represents a step forward.[25] In order to describe what *anti-docetic* might mean, one must first define *docetic*. The word is derived from the Greek verb *dokein*, "to seem." Related to Gnosticism, Docetism was an ancient dualism that equated salvation with escape from the bondage of creation, especially from the body. They did not expect the redemption of creation. In the docetic reading of the gospel, Jesus Christ only appeared to suffer, and someone else (perhaps Simon of Cyrene) took his place on the cross.[26] The writer of 1 John addressed docetic challenges when he insisted,

> Beloved, do not believe every spirit, but test the spirits to see whether they are from God; for many false prophets have gone out into the world. By this you know the Spirit of God: every spirit that confesses

> that Jesus Christ has come in the flesh is from God, and every spirit that does not confess Jesus is not from God. (4:1-3a)

> This is the one who came by water and blood, Jesus Christ, not with the water only but with the water and the blood. (5:6)

There would be no avoiding the embodied (and suffering) Christ. He knew the moral and ethical implications of such a spiritualized gospel, and thus he wrote,

> We know love by this, that he laid down his life for us—and we ought to lay down our lives for one another. How does God's love abide in anyone who has the world's goods and sees a brother or sister in need and yet refuses help? (1 John 3:16-17)

To avoid suffering is to deny the gospel.

Ignatius of Antioch made a similar argument in his early second-century "Letter to the Smyrnaeans" (ca. 115 CE), which he penned en route to his execution in Rome:

> For [Jesus Christ] suffered all these things for our sakes . . . and He suffered truly, as also He raised Himself truly; not as certain Unbelievers say, that He suffered in semblance. . . . For I know and believe that He was in the flesh even after the resurrection.
>
> But mark ye those who hold strange doctrine touching the grace of Jesus Christ which came to us, how that they are contrary to the mind of God. They have no care for love, none for the widow, none for the orphan, none for the afflicted, none for the prisoner, none for the hungry or thirsty. They abstain from eucharist (thanksgiving) and prayer, because they allow not that the eucharist is the flesh of our Saviour Jesus Christ, which flesh suffered for our sins, and which the Father of His goodness raised up.[27]

One can see here the basic theological problem along with its attendant moral and missional failures. According to Ignatius, persons with such a skewed vision of faith "abstained from eucharist and prayer," that is, from the vocational implications of their baptism. Where diakonia died, so did the work of intercession.

While the claim about Christ's escape from the cross did not gain much serious traction in the early church, docetic tendencies continue to challenge the church. We live in a culture that often denies the reality of suffering and death, along with the many challenges and limitations of embodiment. We see docetic tendencies in claims that worship must always be upbeat and worshipers made comfortable. One can also detect a retreat from the cross with funerals that allow little room for lament, and in the trend toward celebrating memorial services without the body present at all.[28] Marjorie Procter-Smith criticizes the "respectful . . . polite . . . benign and moderate tone" found in much church praying, asking, "Where is this benign God when a child is being raped by her father? Where is this powerful God when a woman is beaten or shot to death by her male partner?"[29]

Working from these insights, it has occurred to me that faithful Christian praying must not only avoid the problem of denial, but it must go one step further by intentionally engaging suffering, following Jesus by denying self and taking up the cross (Mark 8:34). In such praying one offers very specific intercessions. One will name suffering and other human struggles in very specific ways—for example, naming "battered spouses" and "victims of bullies" as intercessory foci, along with "endangered species and plants." Such naming does the polar opposite of docetic avoidance, and thus I call these prayers anti-docetic.[30] It is an "in your face" style of interceding, speaking to realities not usually named in polite society. Thinking in terms of the Baptismal Covenant, it enters the dynamics of Christ's dying and rising through active resistance of sin and evil, "in whatever forms they present themselves."[31] And so it looks like the icons and hymns that I have referenced. But what else does it look like? I'll share two narratives, one from a deacon in New Orleans, and further reflections on my friends, the Sisters of the Precious Blood in Dayton, Ohio. I will close the chapter with a set of intercessions that I call "prayers in an anti-docetic mode."

"Like a Vietnam Wall" . . . Remembering the Victims in New Orleans

When I visited St. Anna's Episcopal Church in New Orleans, Louisiana, in mid-March of 2010, I was shown a very simple wall inscribed with dates, names, ages, and grim, one-word reminders of various tragedies: "beaten . . . shot . . . stabbed . . . shot . . . shot . . . beaten." Above the list for 2009 was written an affirmation from the opening words of Psalm 46: "God is our hope and strength, a very present help in trouble." Some persons, like these two from the 2009 list, were listed anonymously, compounding their tragedy:

9/9 John Doe 21 shot
9/14 Jane Doe—beaten

There were three more names between those two unnamed victims, all in chronological order, and four more listed by the twenty-fourth of September. Theirs was a wall of remembrance in the clear but understated style of the Vietnam Veterans Memorial in Washington, D.C. I had learned about the wall, St. Anna's Church, and the work of Deacon Elaine Clements from one of my students.

She was a postulant for ordination when Hurricane Katrina devastated the city in late August 2005. The waters rose, the levees collapsed, and FEMA dithered. Some scattered, some died in their attics,[32] while some others cut holes in their attics and waited on their roofs. The waters receded, but the devastation continued. Clements began her work at St. Anna's in September 2006, a year after Katrina, with an assignment from her diocese to begin an outreach project that would continue after she left nine months later. It was classic diaconal work. During this time, of course, the city was in chaos, and it has been a long slog toward recovery.[33]

Clements noted that when she began her work, the murder rate was essentially two every three days, approximately 250 a year.[34] There was "not enough outrage" about these homicides, she said, and people had come to accept them almost as routine. When I asked her why this was so, she said that many of the victims were perceived as criminal elements. Her rector at St. Anna's, Father Bill Terry, collaborated in the creation of the project, and thus it began. Again, simple signs listed the date of death, name, age, and manner in which each victim died.[35] The wall is anti-docetic, a conscientious refusal to forget or otherwise cover the grim fact. It is a focused and nonviolent expression of outrage.

The memorial wall was but one part of the effort. In memory of each victim, they also gave roses to the mayor, the chief of police, members of the city council, and the district attorney's office. At first, she said, the DA's office was quite suspicious. When given the roses, "they acted like it was a bomb." The police asked, "Don't you think we know about this?" She assured them that they had given the flowers as a sign of the church's intent to stand with them in their struggle. In a sense, they were a sign of their intercessions for the police.

When Deacon Clements moved on from St. Anna's Church, she remained involved in a wider effort to promote the church's intercession on behalf of the murder victims. At St. Anna's, the names for the entire year were read on All Souls' day (November 2) and also on Good Friday, with the latter making a particularly clear connection between the suffering of the victims and that of Jesus. To stand with one is to stand with the other. At the time of our interview, she estimated that about twenty churches in the diocese were offering such prayers, although it is hard to know how many have continued the practice. Nevertheless, it presents an impressive testimony as to how the church might respond to a crisis.

Given the structure of the prayers, names of the murder victims were sometimes read alongside the names of those who have died within the parish, a potentially controversial juxtaposition. The best way to avoid such tension, however, is to avoid specificity, but her commitment to her work as deacon was too conscientious for that. Offering bland prayers in the face of such devastation should be as incomprehensible as offering generic relief ministry in the same place. Both must be specific. Part of our interview took place outside St. Anna's as we looked at the wall, but a large part of it took place as we drove through the Ninth Ward in her pickup truck. On that morning in March 2010, "only 11 percent of the residents had returned." As she described it, the neighborhood before Katrina had been poor, but full of energy. Many would sit outside their houses and interact in the streets, "because that was more interesting than sitting in their dark shotgun houses." "Before Katrina," said Deacon Elaine, "if you wanted to build a new house, you had to buy an old one and tear it down first," but now much of the space was empty. "Anywhere that you see green, there had been a house there before." She showed me houses with X's painted on them, which meant that they had been searched for bodies in the months following Katrina. I saw other houses with holes cut in the roofs, including the one from which Fats Domino had been rescued. The holes in the roofs meant that some had cut their way to temporary safety on the roofs, but they were also grim reminders of those who had drowned in similar attics or perished slowly in the post-Katrina heat and humidity. One cannot pray generically amid such a landscape. And so, on a weekly basis, she brought that neighborhood into dialogue with the classic agenda for prayers of the people as laid out in *The Book of Common Prayer* (1979):

> The Universal Church, its members, and its mission
> The Nation and all in authority
> The welfare of the world
> The concerns of the local community
> Those who suffer and those in any trouble
> The departed (with commemoration of a saint when appropriate)[36]

This classic prayer agenda, which is not much different from the ancient Good Friday prayers noted earlier, represents broad ecumenical consensus.[37] If the church were to start over again, we might come to a similar list—even the emerging practice of praying for the environment can be understood under prayers for the welfare of the world. In her context, Deacon Elaine took that broad and comprehensive agenda and made it specific, as in the following prayer offered for the world:

> For the world and its leaders and people, especially for people whose homes were lost in the mudslides of Haiti and in the flooding in Mexico City; for the families of the hundreds of people killed in the ferry accidents in Sierra Leone and in the Philippines and for all those killed this week by bombings and air strikes in Afghanistan and Iraq. Help us open our hearts to the needs of others. Let us pray to the Lord. Hear our prayer.[38]

The specificity evinced dialogue with the events of the week, and the reference to those killed by the bombings and air strikes in Afghanistan and Iraq was a particularly bold move to make within an American congregation. By the definition that we have established here, however, even the suffering of enemies is the suffering of Christ, and to avoid the realities of war—like dead people as collateral damage and even the flag-draped caskets of American soldiers—is docetic spirituality at its most insidious. On the other hand, naming it resists both avoidance and the violence that it covers.

A British Petroleum oil spill that occurred in the Gulf of Mexico in late spring of 2010 was devastating in its own way, once again calling forth Deacon Clements' intercessory compassion and imagination. When I asked her how she was praying in the face of the spill, I was surprised to hear her say, "It was worse than Katrina by far. . . . This spill has the potential to destroy every aspect of our economy: fishing, oil, tourism, and shipping."[39] Regardless of how one ranks it, the church is called to look directly at such suffering, naming it and offering it to God, and thus she offered this prayer for the Gulf, its people, and even its creatures:

> Most especially today we pray for our Gulf, being contaminated with untold thousands of barrels of oil. Watch over those who are working to lessen the massive environmental damage and to stop the leaking oil. Bring comfort to our fishermen and all who make their living from the sea in their fears about loss of livelihood. Watch over the sea creatures living in the waters and our fragile marshes, home to so much precious life. Holy Spirit, guide us to protect your creation and grant us the ability to continue to hope.[40]

Such praying is anti-docetic both in its specificity and in its grappling with suffering. The prayers offered by those who have been buried with Christ in baptism should move in this direction.

Sisters of the Precious Blood, Salem Heights, Ohio, and Their Ecumenical Friends

In the first chapter I told the story of Sisters Canice Werner and Dorothy Kammerer, who looked at murder rates in Dayton and stated the proverbial "Someone ought to do something." They realized that God was calling them, and so the street vigils began. The vigils developed into an ecumenical effort with ownership widely felt among the community and partner churches. We heard about one of the early events, when the two sisters and their companions were challenged in the middle of the street and persisted in moving to the place of prayer. Movement to the place of prayer and gathering there remains a major part of the liturgy, an enacted refusal to cede the streets to violence and fear. As one witness said, "Many times when we gather blood is still staining the ground."[41] As a further act of resistance, it embodies a refusal to forget either the neighborhood or the individuals who have died, "for the blood of each person is precious."[42]

That value resonates deeply within the anti-docetic piety of the sisters. As I said in another place, disciples of Jesus Christ cannot grow faint at the sight of blood,[43] and there is certainly none of that with the Sisters of the Precious Blood. For them, there is no separating the blood of Jesus and the blood of each human being. Each is precious. Note this prayer used at one of their vigils, which draws upon imagery in the biblical story of Cain and Abel, the archetypal murder story (Gen. 4):

> God of life, source of our hope:
> The violence within our world, our communities, our families, indeed with our very selves is destroying Your creation.
> In union with the Precious Blood of Jesus give us the strength to break

the cycle of violence, to hear the cry of the Blood
and make sacred again Your Earth stained by Blood![44]

The prayer speaks to the interconnection between all human blood, the sacramental Blood of Jesus, and the lifeblood of all creation. It refuses to look away from that blood, from the cross itself, but not because of any morbid fascination. It seeks, rather, to save us from further waste. To do so, we must regard each drop as precious.

A hymn often used at the vigils expresses these themes in an equally clear-eyed and graphic way, connecting the blood of Jesus to the blood of the poor:

The blood of Jesus refreshes our souls
Gives us new courage, liberates our lives
The blood of the poor soaks into the land,
Cries out for justice, yearning for peace.

Refrain:
We are redeemed in the blood of Christ. We are washed in love.
Sent by the blood, stained by the blood, we are servants of the blood of Christ.[45]

Their work is rooted in this piety, and it has shaped responses like the street vigils and their protests against the death penalty, but it is not theirs alone. For those willing to hear it, theirs is the piety of the Bible, and thus it should be shared by all Christians.

Indeed, their witness has led to an extensive network. As Sister Donna Liette described it to me in 2010, when a homicide occurred in Dayton, Trotwood, or Harrison Township, she went to the neighborhood and tried to find a suitable place where parking was available and where persons could stand and pray. Then she notified the media and the police, who gave protection and sometimes closed down the street for the time of the vigil. When these arrangements were settled, they sent out a simple e-mail to the community of vigil participants, announcing the details.[46] Although Sister Donna has moved to another assignment within their order, the process remains as it was.

An average group of about twenty to twenty-five persons gathers on any given Saturday, although the entire vigil community numbers around one hundred. A sense of community has developed among them, and so those who do not attend on a particular Saturday are aware that others are praying.[47] As I describe it in chapter 3, what matters most is not that a particular person is praying, but that the whole church prays. Many of them have come to cherish the relationships developed in this work, although they remain deeply aware of the circumstances that bring them together. As one minister said, "We say to each other, 'See you next time, but hopefully not too soon.' "[48]

It was never just the sisters. As Sister Jeanette Buehler related to me, early in the process a group of young African American men saw "these little old white ladies" coming into their neighborhoods to pray and knew that they needed to do something. The Street Souljahz began to join the vigils.[49] As one of their members told me, many of these men come from troubled neighborhoods, and some have been in prison, but all of them are Christians "who have turned their lives around."[50] The Souljahz wear yellow shirts at public events like the vigils, so their presence is visible. They are "sprinkled in" to the gathering to be helpful, for positive conversation "but not to bash people over the head with our Bibles."[51] The Souljahz encourage people to come to the vigils, Sister Donna had told me, but "they also protect us."[52] It is possible that there could be danger in offering witness such as the vigils, but this has not been the experience of the vigil members. Nevertheless, it is not work for the faint of heart.

What is the shape of their prayer? The vigils are held at noon on Saturdays, and the liturgy follows this simple, ecumenically adaptable pattern:

- They begin with a prayer or a song.
- Scripture is read (something like the story of Cain killing Abel, or some other text chosen by the leader, depending on the circumstances).
- Reflections are offered focusing on the life of the victim. Sometimes family members, friends, and/or neighbors will speak.
- Intercessory prayer is offered.
- The family is given a seven-day candle bearing the name of the deceased.[53]

It is simple but profound witness, with the style of the service influenced by the group assigned to lead it during that month. Indeed, some of the more evangelical African American groups don't necessarily want to use the "cooked prayers" of the Catholics, but they've learned from each other.[54] The movement to the place of prayer and the gathering on that spot is much more important than any particular prayer, reading, or hymn that might be offered. I count myself fortunate that I did not have opportunity to witness one of the street vigils, but instead talked with some of the participants and toured some neighborhoods where they have been held.

How does this practice of keeping vigils shape those who participate in it, especially the leaders? We made a discovery together during the conversation that I had with some of them during my March 2012 visit. My primary host, Sister Jeanette, scheduled a group interview/conversation that involved a local priest, a minister from an independent church, several of the sisters, a chaplain from the county jail, and a local justice activist, as well as the person who sends the e-mails announcing the vigils. All knew one another from participation in the vigils, and all were busy. The type of person who carves out time for the vigils does so because she or he is committed to the work, not because the person doesn't have many other things to do. I shared my own ambivalence in scheduling a time to visit them. I had known about their work for more than two years and had wanted to visit, but I wasn't sure what I was asking for. Was I, at some level, hoping for a murder so that I could come and watch the liturgical response to it? Once I could name that ambivalence, I was able to request the visit and schedule it, and I told them that I was truly glad that we could have our late morning conversation on a Saturday, because it meant that there had been no murder that week, and thus there would be no homicide vigil.

I asked them to tell me about the vigils and why they participate in them, and they shared with me many of the things that I have already noted here. They witness to give hope, so that violence does not get the last word. They gather because they believe in justice. They witness because of the fellowship that they share with one another. It is interdenominational, interracial, and intergenerational, and they cherish those relationships. They witness because the practice is part of their continuing conversion, for they, also, could be tempted to see some deaths as less than significant. Participating in the vigils and hearing the testimonies helped them see that the victim was always "someone's mother . . . someone's son." As they shared about these gatherings for prayer, various ones of them echoed the refrain, "I wish we could do more." In and around that lament, we heard other stories. A school principal asked his students whether they had relatives in jail, or whether they had been touched by homicide, and two-thirds of them answered yes. He began to relate to them in a new way.

The vigils themselves were not merely the speaking of words. We heard of a woman who came to a vigil broken by the thought that she should have done more for the victim. She was surrounded and embraced, and so neglect (perceived or real) and the accompanying guilt did not get the final word. We heard that the street vigils were the only public remembrances spoken for many of the victims. And so the conversation deepened. One participant remained relatively quiet through much of the hour, but then with quavering voice, he said, "We say, 'What more can we do?' But look at what we are doing?" In that moment, they realized that they had given themselves a gift by gathering for conversation. Later, I heard from others who had formed support groups for survivors and their families.[55]

So then, what more can we do? It is a common lament for those who pray with persistence, especially when violence and pain continue. What good does it do? Worse than that, is praying itself an act of naive avoidance? When prayer is done honestly, standing with the crucified Jesus as the participants in the homicide vigils do, the intercessions of our mouths almost always lead to other forms of embodied intercession. There is no need to choose which form of intercession we will do, for each seems to lead to the other.

I commend the anti-docetic work of these sisters and brothers in New Orleans and Dayton. There are places where similar prayers could be offered, and likely some near you. Not long ago I visited El Mozote, a small village in the remote mountains of Morazan province in El Salvador. On December 11, 1981, government troops, funded by United States tax dollars, massacred an entire village—men, women, children, babies, and the elderly. One woman, Rufina Amaya, escaped to hide, and later she told the story of the massacre.

Even then few believed it until a team of Argentine forensic anthropologists confirmed her story in 1992.[56] A renewed village has emerged there, while memorial ruins have been preserved. In the midst stands a simple monument bearing the names of those who were massacred. Again, the place of the cross is marked and the faithful refuse to ignore it. Can we? As I learned the story, I realized that Rufina's infant son, torn from her breast on the day of the massacre, had been about the same age as my son, who was born the previous December. I think also of a woman whose partner lost a son to a brutal suicide on a railroad track, thereby ending a life beset by drug and alcohol abuse and depression, patterns that developed long before an underlying autism spectrum disorder was diagnosed. Eventually, the woman and her partner went to pray at that site, both for their own healing and also to speak a better word than despair.[57]

These stories and the intercessions that accompany them address death, but remember the broad range of suffering that we identified with the biblical Passion narratives. To stand beneath the cross with the suffering Jesus is to intercede in the midst of many painful circumstances. The following set of intercessions, prepared for the 2011 Retreat of the Order of Saint Luke, illustrates this dynamic and should bring the dynamic of anti-docetic praying a bit closer to home.

Intercessions in an Anti-Docetic Mode[58]

The Prayer Text

I ask your prayers for Creation:
    for lands stripped of trees.
    for polluted water and air.
    for endangered species and plants.
Pray for Creation.
    (Silence)
Hear us, O God.
Kyrie, Kyrie, Eleison

I ask your prayers for the nations of the world and their peoples:
for those troubled by war and violent conflict.
for economic justice among the nations.
for the will to use earth's resources wisely.
Pray for the nations.
(Silence)
Hear us, O God.
Kyrie, Kyrie, Eleison.

I ask your prayers for the welfare of this region:
for those who commute to work, that they do so gently and with patience.
for all workers, especially those who work outdoors in difficult weather.
For shalom among racial and ethnic groups, and among persons of differing sexual orientation.
Pray for the people of the Dallas–Fort Worth region.
(Silence)
Hear us, O God.
Kyrie, Kyrie, Eleison.

I ask your prayers for the Church:
for victims of sexual abuse and underpaid employees.
for overworked pastors and volunteers.
for the healing of divisions within Christ's Body.
Pray for the Church.
(Silence)
Hear us, O God.
Kyrie, Kyrie, Eleison.

I ask your prayers for those who suffer, and those in need:
for those with cancer and heart disease, and all who need healing.
for those without food or shelter.
for battered spouses.

for victims of other violent crimes and their families.
for prisoners, especially those awaiting execution.
for estranged children, parents, and in-laws.
for children troubled by bullies.
Pray for those who suffer and those in need.
(Silence)
Hear us, O God.
Kyrie, Kyrie, Eleison.

I ask your prayers for those who have died, especially these whom we name before you.
(Naming of the faithful)
(Silence)
Hear us, O God.
Kyrie, Kyrie, Eleison.

I invite you to speak other prayers and petitions.
(Pause while prayers are spoken)
Hear us, O God.
Kyrie, Kyrie, Eleison.

O Lord our God, accept the fervent prayers of your people; in the multitude of your mercies, look with compassion upon us and all who turn to you for help; for you are gracious, O lover of souls, and to you we give glory, Father, Son, and Holy Spirit, now and for ever. *Amen.*[59]

Structural Logic

I organized these intercessions according to a biddings structure similar to that offered in *The Book of Common Prayer* (1979), Form II for the Prayers of the People.[60] While very specific intercessory foci are named, such as prayers for victims of bullies, these are subsumed under the wider categories that we noted earlier: church, nation, world, local community, those who suffer, and the departed.[61] I added prayers for creation, an area of intercessory focus that I am convinced reflects an emerging sense of the faithful that we should articulate and that we will explore further within the next chapter. As noted earlier, these classic categories encourage leaders of corporate prayers to transcend lists of "joys and concerns" that focus primarily on parochial concerns.

An essential aspect of this set of intercessions is the silence provided after each bidding. These periods of silence afford individuals within the assembly some free space in which to process the specific intercessions. Such specificity is characteristic of the anti-docetic mode; nevertheless, it can be difficult to process, and the silence provides space for doing so. The prayer leader was instructed to allow the silence to continue for at least thirty seconds after the speaking of each bidding, and slightly longer if he or she she thought it both necessary and helpful. The leader ended the silence by saying, "Hear us, O God," and thus set the pace for the prayers. These and other prayers of the people are best led an unhurried manner. A *kyrie*[62] provided a way for the assembly to make a unison response in a classic form.

Intercessory forms best proceed when they follow a clear structure that allows for corporate prayers with a comprehensive reach. They should also provide a place for persons to speak petitions aloud, indeed, to raise their particular joys and concerns. Over time, praying in a more comprehensive, anti-docetic mode will encourage participants to bring with them a wider array of such personal concerns, not to mention thanksgivings. Within the form offered here, space for such individually spoken prayers occurs before the concluding collect.

The list of concerns that I have included in these biddings is not exhaustive. Because that is always the case, local churches should spend time discerning the shape and content of their public prayers, following classic forms but presuming that they are incomplete. As always, many other specific concerns could have been named, and congregations that adapt forms such as these should not hesitate to add them. The open space within the form itself, however, allows a congregation to edit them in the moment. Such expansion is always the local church's privilege, if not its responsibility. Pastors, worship leaders, and assemblies of the faithful must continue working at the anti-docetic task; otherwise, they will likely revert to avoidance and irrelevance in their praying.

And so we have prayed under the shadow of the cross, and that is difficult work, although necessary. As we will explore in the next chapter, the Baptismal Covenant also calls us to pray within the dynamics of repentance. As we will see, this means making an imaginative turn toward the reign of God.

CHAPTER SIX

Intercession and the Baptismal Covenant

Turning Toward the Reign of God

The call to repent is a primary emphasis within the baptismal covenant. We ask the question, "Do you renounce the spiritual forces of wickedness, reject the evil powers of this world, and repent of your sin?"[1] which is rooted in the earliest biblical accounts of baptismal practice. John the Baptist proclaimed, "Repent, for the kingdom of heaven has come near" (Matt. 3:2). On the Day of Pentecost, Peter addressed those who were "cut to the heart" by his sermon, telling them, "Repent, and be baptized every one of you in the name of Jesus Christ so that your sins may be forgiven; and you will receive the gift of the Holy Spirit" (Acts 2:37-38). What do we mean by this word *repent*, and what does it have to do with our project of developing a baptismal theology for the church's intercessory work? In order to examine this question, we will turn to the witness of John the Baptist and his ministry in the Judean wilderness. While John the Baptist may seem an unlikely guide, when we listen to him carefully we discover that he can point us to a broader and deeper practice of prayer, even to dreams of the reign of God.

John the Baptist, the Call to Metanoia, and Dreams of the Reign of God

Listen to this narrative of John's ministry from Matthew's Gospel:

> In those days John the Baptist appeared in the wilderness of Judea, proclaiming, "Repent, for the kingdom of heaven has come near." This is the one of whom the prophet Isaiah spoke when he said,
>
> "The voice of one crying out in the wilderness: 'Prepare the way of the Lord, make his paths straight.' "
>
> Now John wore clothing of camel's hair with a leather belt around his waist, and his food was locusts and wild honey. Then the people of Jerusalem and all Judea were going out to him, and all the region along the Jordan, and they were baptized by him in the river Jordan, confessing their sins. (Matt. 3:1-6)

Again, how does this text contribute to our ongoing discussion of intercessory prayer in relation to baptism? The narrative of John the Baptist, of course, is important to Christians because his witness led to the baptism of Jesus (Matt. 3:13-17).

First, however, notice that the Gospel text places John "in the wilderness" (Matt. 3:1). How does that matter? Within the biblical narrative, "wilderness" is a desolate space, frightening and challenging because of its emptiness. One can, however, perceive that reality in a different way, viewing emptiness as an open space. And so, in the history of Israel the wilderness was a place of possibilities. In many ways, the wilderness was the place of their spiritual birth, where they were formed as a people. In the wilderness, God led them to freedom through the Red Sea waters (Exod. 14). In the wilderness, God led them by "the pillar of cloud by day" and "the pillar of fire by night" (Exod. 13:22). God fed them with manna, "bread from heaven" (Exod. 16:4), and also quenched their thirst with water from the rock (Exod. 17:1-7). In the wilderness, God gave them the Law (Exod. 19–20 and following), and they also learned hard lessons of faith that perhaps could be received nowhere else (Exod. 32). Their ritual life began to take shape in the wilderness, under the tabernacle, where God's presence was revealed in the midst of a tent that was moved when the people moved (Exod. 25–31; 35–40). One could argue that ritual life fared better in the wilderness than it ever did in the seeming permanence of the Temple, where it eventually became allied with monarchical power and its injustices.[2] Nevertheless, in times of corruption and decline the wilderness called again. When the prophet Elijah was discouraged and fearing for his life, he went back to Mount Horeb, to the place where Moses had met God and received the Commandments, and there he had a clarifying encounter with God, and from there returned to his ministry (1 Kings 19:1-18). Given this narrative, then, for a Jewish listener the wilderness is not just a foreboding and empty place, it is a place of possibility, of new beginnings and dreams. It is a strangely positive place, and this emphasis remains for Christians.

As we know, Jesus went to the wilderness following his baptism, "led up by the Spirit into the wilderness to be tempted by the devil" (Matt. 4:1-2). Emerging from that encounter, Jesus began his work of teaching and healing. Notice that the Gospel writer summarized Jesus' proclamation using the exact words attributed to John the Baptist in chapter 3: "Repent, for the kingdom of heaven has come near" (Matt. 4:17), and the repetition is significant, another link between God's covenant with Israel and the New Covenant. And so the emphasis continues. Each Lent, the church reenters a spiritual wilderness, encountering its challenges while also seeking its unique benefits. We don't reenter the wilderness as some odd sort of punishment for our sins; rather, we go there to regain focus for our discipleship. Led by this text, we will consider the wilderness as a place of dreaming, but first we need to move to the heart of the matter, to the deeper meaning of *repent*, that word used by both John the Baptist and Jesus, and now, by the church.

Our English word is translated from the Greek *metanoia.* It occurs in both noun (repentance) and verb (repent) forms, in the context both of John the Baptist's preaching (Matt. 3:2, 8) and throughout the New Testament (Luke 5:32; 15:7; Acts 11:18; 20:21; Rom. 2:4, etc.). Literally, *metanoia* means a change of mind or change of thought (*meta-nous*), and thus to do metanoia is to make a turn, to move from one way of thinking and acting to another. Often, Christians have emphasized the first part of this movement, the turn away from sin, away from that which diminishes and destroys life. That emphasis is well expressed in the text before us: "They were baptized by him in the river Jordan, confessing their sins" (Matt. 3:6). One also finds it expressed in the narrative that follows, in which John the Baptist rebukes the religious leaders, calling them a "brood of vipers" subject to the wrath of God. He demands that they "bear fruit worthy of repentance [metanoia]" (Matt. 3:7-8). Even here, the idea of fruit points to a life-giving result that will emerge.

However, classic liturgical texts have kept our focus on repentance as the turn away from sin. Note, for instance, the following prayer that first appeared in the 1549 version of The Book of Common Prayer

> We acknowledge and bewail our manifold sins and wickedness, which we from time to time most grievously have committed, by thought, word and deed, against thy divine majesty, provoking most justly thy wrath and indignation against us, we do earnestly repent and are heartily sorry for these our misdoings, the remembrance of them is grievous unto us, the burden of them is intolerable.

It remains in Anglican sources to this day, with close variants in Methodism,[3] and on the surface I have no argument with its claims. Only when we realize that sin is an intolerable burden can we decisively renounce it as the Baptismal Covenant demands. As this prayer moves toward its conclusion, it does, in fact, point toward serving and pleasing God in "newness of life," but not with the same energy expended on its language about sin.

In like manner, the Prayer of Humble Access is a well-known classic form within the same Anglican-Methodist tradition, beginning with the 1549 Book of Common Prayer:

> We do not presume to come to this thy table, merciful Lord, trusting in our own righteousness, but in thy manifold and great mercies: We be not worthy to gather up the crumbs under thy table: But thou art the same Lord whose property is always to have mercy.[4]

The prayer then asks for the blessing of full participation in the sacramental table, which, we may presume, is granted. As with the aforementioned confession, this prayer is a brilliant piece of liturgical literature. We are not worthy of God's gifts, not even the crumbs under the table. That is not, of course, the final point. Those who recognize the biblical background of this prayer—the encounter between Jesus and a Canaanite woman who came on behalf of her tormented daughter (Matt. 15:21-28)—know that Jesus, moved by her great faith, gave her not just a few crumbs, but he granted her petition in full, healing her daughter. Both became participants in God's blessing, in the reign of God, and those who commune receive the same blessings (Matt. 15:27-28).

Nevertheless, the contemporary ritual revisions of the Eucharist within The Episcopal Church (USA), and The United Methodist Church did not retain this prayer.[5] The problem with the Prayer of Humble Access was not so much its content as it was the sense that it was a doubling of confession. In the previous rites, the "we acknowledge and bewail" preceded the Great Thanksgiving, and the Prayer of Humble Access followed it, and that in concert with the *Agnus Dei* ("O Lamb of God"), which made its own thrice-repeated plea for mercy in the face of our sin.[6] How many times must one say it? In the Western Catholic tradition inherited by Anglicans and Methodists, and retained in many other Protestant churches, the answer to that question would be, "Many times."[7]

Our problem, then, is not so much in the content and form of such prayers, but rather in the unbalanced manner in which we have heard and used them. Eliminating or suppressing prayers of confession is not a wise move; they are necessary, although perhaps in moderation, and when used they should be strongly and specifically worded. We need to understand, however, that our heavily penitential Western tradition, along with the individualistic understanding of salvation that has accompanied it, has made it difficult for us to hear the positive dynamics in metanoia. Often overlooked in the ever-persistent "[bewailing of] our manifold sins and wickedness" is the affirmation that neither we nor creation is doomed to remain stuck in its effects.

We can make the turn from sin toward the reign of God, and that is God's dream for us. We hear it in the second movement of John's call: "Repent, *for the kingdom of heaven has come near*" (Matt. 3:2, emphasis added). Our English word *kingdom* is translated from the Greek *basilea*, which may also be translated "reign." Kingdom, of course, may evoke problematic associations, perhaps of autocratic men who receive tribute and dispatch young subjects to fight their battles. In this use of "kingdom," we have here another instance of New Testament writers taking a common term and breaking it toward a new meaning shaped by Christ and the gospel.[8] As King, Christ reigns not from a throne room but from the cross, and one finds audience with him in the wilderness. As with *metanoia*, translating *basilea* as "reign" can help us to hear the text in a different way.

When they call us to repent with eyes looking toward God's reign, John (and Jesus) call us not so much to introspective sorrow as to the aligning of our bodies with what God is doing. This is metanoia at its fullest. And so we might finally hear the invitation in this way: "Turn, for the reign of God has come near." That which comes next in Matthew 3 supports such a reading:

> This is the one of whom the prophet Isaiah spoke when he said,
> "The voice of one crying out in the wilderness:
> 'Prepare the way of the Lord,
> make his paths straight.'" (Matt. 3:3)

We hear this quotation from Isaiah 40:3, but the reference invites us to consider the wider context of Isaiah 40, especially verses 3-5, with its vision of uneven ground made level and the glory of the Lord revealed. Here is holy imagination, rendered deep and broad:

> A voice cries out:
> "In the wilderness prepare the way of the LORD,
> make straight in the desert a highway for our God.
> Every valley shall be lifted up,
> and every mountain and hill be made low;
> the uneven ground shall become level,

and the rough places a plain.
Then the glory of the Lord shall be revealed.
and all the people shall see it together
for the mouth of the Lord has spoken." (Isa. 40:3-5)

One hears more such visions throughout Isaiah 40 of God as a shepherd who feeds the flock and gently leads it (v. 11), of a God "who brings princes to naught, and makes the rulers of the earth as nothing" (v. 23). Those who learn to depend upon this God will find their strength renewed; "they shall run and not be weary" (Isa. 40:31). Indeed, Isaiah 40 presents the great dream given to the children of Israel during their Babylonian captivity. In like manner, it is a dream given to all who yearn for God's liberating work.

Through the witness of John the Baptist, the reader is invited to continue in it, and indeed, we are commanded to do so: "Repent, for the kingdom of heaven has come near. . . . Prepare the way of the Lord" (Matt. 3:2-3). So then, there is much in this passage that links metanoia to the turn from sin (Matt. 3:5-10), but there is something else here as well, this call to envision God's future. Both movements are necessary, and both should lead us deeper into the dynamics of intercession.

What Does That Look Like? What Does God Want?

What does the reign of God look like? What does God want? Do we dare ask such questions?

We should ask such questions, all the while guarding against making wrongful use of God's name (Exod. 20:7). That we might make such wrongful use is always a danger in preaching, teaching, and writing about matters of the Spirit.[9] The best way to avoid such harm is to remain in close dialogue with the poetic and prophetic visions of the scriptures, yet even that reading must remain in conversation with the ways of Jesus as we encounter them in the Gospels. Then all must be discerned within the body of Christ, with each member of the church given his or her rightful voice within the whole. With such safeguards in our practice, it is less likely that demagogues will influence the church toward harmful and destructive ends, but we must dream, even if we sometimes miss the mark. If God's people had not dreamed about what God wants for the world, segregation might remain legal within the United States, and child labor laws may never have been written. Neither result was inevitable. There is, of course, much more dreaming yet to be done, and it begins to take shape in the church's intercessory prayers. What does such praying look like? I will begin to address that question by providing two negative examples. They show what intercessory prayer can sound like when it fails to engage in that first movement in metanoia, the turn away from sin.

I encountered this dynamic, oddly enough perhaps, in several instances while reading Thomas L. Friedman's book *Hot, Flat, and Crowded: Why We Need a Green Revolution, and How It Can Renew America.*[10] Every year, our Southern Methodist University provost encourages the faculty to attend the spring term General Faculty Meeting by giving us a book at the end of his presentation, and it is a good way to draw academicians to a meeting. Friedman's book was the Provost's choice for 2009. Friedman is not, of course, a theologian, but rather a Pulitzer Prize–winning columnist with the *New York Times*. He argues that America needs to change its energy consumption and carbon usage habits, and that it should lead the world in doing so. Such change, he insists, would make good sense not only ecologically, but also economically.[11] There are not, he insists, two sides on the global warming issue, given that we have seen dramatic increases in levels of CO_2 in the last fifty years "from 284 ppm [parts per million] to 384 ppm."[12] He suggests, by the way, that "global weirding" might be a better term to bring to the discussion, since the effect of climate change is not merely higher temperatures, but the skewing of patterns toward extremes.[13] As usual with the provost's choices, *Hot, Flat, and Crowded* made for an interesting and provocative read.

To reiterate, Friedman is not a theologian. On the other hand, I am one, a liturgical theologian to be precise, and I bring that lens to everything I read.[14] Therefore, I noticed when Friedman discussed two politicians who had recently called their constituents to pray for rain in the midst of extreme drought conditions. The first happened in Australia. Friedman reported,

> I visited Australia in May 2007, and found myself in the middle of what Aussies were calling the "Big Dry," a roughly seven-year drought that had become so severe that on April 19, 2007, then Prime Minister John Howard actually asked his countrymen to put their hands together and beseech the Good Lord for a gully-washing downpour. Because if it didn't start to pour, said Howard, he was going to have to ban water allocations for irrigation purposes in the Murray-Darling river basin, which produces 40 percent of Australia's agriculture. That would be like an Egyptian pharaoh banning irrigation from the Nile or a U.S. President from the Mississippi.[15]

Friedman went on to describe how calling for such prayer was, in fact, a key part of Howard's response to the Big Dry. In the meantime, Friedman noted, Howard had refused to lead Australia into ratification of the Kyoto Protocol, a United Nations effort to address the actual causes of climate change. That failure, he posited, was a primary reason for Howard's subsequent defeat at the polls.[16]

In like manner, Friedman described a prayer vigil called by Georgia governor Sonny Perdue in response to a record-breaking drought in his state. The praying took place on the Georgia capitol steps. According to Friedman, Perdue did acknowledge his state's "wastefulness."[17] Even so, he reported, *Time* magazine took Perdue to task in its November 19, 2007, issue, "for relying too much on the Good Lord and not enough on common sense":

> It wasn't God who allowed an outdoor theme park to build a million-gallon mountain of snow while the Southeast was running dry; it was Governor Perdue and his elected officials. . . . They also allowed the wasteful irrigation of Georgia's cotton farms and the rampant overbuilding and overslurping of metropolitan Atlanta.[18]

It seems that Perdue also laid blame for Atlanta's water shortage on the Endangered Species Act, which attempts to protect the health of Florida rivers and the species that depend upon them. Thus, Friedman also quoted Florida author Diane Roberts, who challenged Governor Perdue: "I'm all for prayer. I'm for rain dances, Santeria chicken sacrifice, Wiccan weather spells or any other magic that might coax H_2O from heaven." But, she insisted, don't blame the Endangered Species Act.[19]

One cannot help but notice the sarcasm expressed in these critiques—the "Good Lord" language and the "put your hands together" phrase, as well as lumping Christian prayer in with chicken sacrifices. As a Christian committed to the prayer of the church, hearing such things is not easy. One could dismiss them as confirmation of a mainstream media's bias (even hostility) against faith practices. But these prayers deserved this criticism. As I noted earlier, Friedman is not a theologian, and he does not use the language of repentance and metanoia. Nevertheless, he seemed to know intuitively that something essential was missing from the prayers of these politicians. Metanoia was that missing piece. As we have established, *metanoia* means "to turn around," literally to turn from sin toward God and God's ways. The problem, then, is not so much the praying for rain, but rather the making of such prayers without changing one's behavior. Metanoia is something that we do, not merely words that we speak. We cannot rightly expect God to fix a problem that we caused without us doing something as well, without discerning God's vision for the future and trying to align ourselves with it, however haltingly. This is what John the Baptist meant when he challenged the religious leaders to "bear fruit worthy [*axios*] of repentance" (Matt. 3:8). One could also understand that phrase to mean, "Bear fruit corresponding to (or consistent with) repentance." And so, as we discussed in chapter 4, adequate prayer begins not so much with our words, but with our actions. Without beginning a turn in our behavior, the spoken bewailing of sin is presumptuous. Without metanoia, we miss the blessing of participating in God's redeeming work.

Metanoia and Praying with Creation

Perhaps, then, Friedman is a theologian after all. Prophetic words often emerge in unexpected places, from persons who do not have particularly good things to say about our religious practices. Amos provides a well-known example of this dynamic:

I hate, I despise your festivals,
  and I take no delight in your solemn assemblies. . . .
Take away from me the noise of your songs;
  I will not listen to the melody of your harps.
But let justice roll down like waters,
  and righteousness like an ever-flowing stream. (Amos 5:21, 23-24)

Friedman's criticism of the prayers stands within that tradition, but he also brings a gentler, more invitational word. He described attending a seminar where "environmental pioneer" Amory Lovins was making a presentation. Someone asked him, "What is the single most important thing an environmentalist can do today?"

> He answered with two words: "Pay attention." Because when you really see it, you'll want to save it.[20]

Friedman continued by describing a visit that he and his family took to the Peruvian rain forest, with a guide who was able to notice "every chirp, whistle, howl, or crackle in the rain forest."[21] Through him, they were able to see, hear, and appreciate much more than they would have done otherwise. While one may not be able to afford such travel, one may be able to do a similar noticing much closer to home, perhaps even in one's backyard.

Thinking along these lines, my favorite place for writing is the table on our back patio, and I work there whenever my schedule and the Texas weather will allow it. When I'm there, I notice the squirrels that move from our live oak tree onto our fence, and from there onto our roof, constantly in motion. I can watch the blue jays that visit and stake out various territorial claims, sometimes against cardinals who dare to visit. I like to see the cardinals, but the jays usually chase them off, and it's their battle, not mine. We keep several flowerpots on the patio, which attract bees and other insects. Our flowerpots also serve as an occasional hiding place for a collection of geckos. One day, a hard rain had left several inches of water in a candleholder that sat on the patio table. As I wrote, I suddenly noticed that one of the geckos had climbed onto the table, bold perhaps, or else oblivious to my presence. I watched as it surveyed the scene and then moved across the table, amid my papers and books, climbed into the candleholder, and found the water. Noticing the gecko's quest was good for me. I cannot say exactly how that was the case—in many ways watching his journey was simply fun—but I sense that somehow I am more open to what God is doing in the world when I take the time to notice such things. At the least, I realize that I'm not the only inhabitant of our yard, that our ownership of space is temporary and tentative. The blue jays might agree with that assessment.[22]

I will now move our attention several hundred miles beyond our patio. In March of 2010, I spent an afternoon walking in the Barataria Preserve while in New Orleans to visit Deacon Elliott and the prayer wall at St. Anna's. The preserve is part of the local bayou, part of the Jean Lafitte National Park and Preserve, located in various sites in and around the city. I was on an alligator quest that afternoon, never having seen one in the wild, and we were told that the warm and sunny early spring day was ideal for viewing gators, and so it was. During our four-mile walk we were rewarded with about ten sightings of alligators, some moving in the water and others on the ground near it. Anyone who has spent much time in National Parks knows the basic rules for viewing wildlife: (1) Stay on the path (in this case, a wooden boardwalk); and (2) observe the wildlife, but don't interfere with them. It is, after all, their habitat, and they are neither pets nor zoo animals.

In the course of our walk, we encountered a youth group, perhaps in town to do post-Katrina relief work. We watched as one of the adolescent boys in the group began throwing sticks at an alligator that, in his opinion, wasn't moving quickly enough. At the moment, the gator wasn't moving at all. I was stunned, and perhaps especially because his adult chaperone seemed in no hurry to make him stop. Besides being dangerous, his behavior was more evidence of a widespread and serious alienation from creation. We can, by God's grace, turn from that alienation toward something better. At the least we should notice our fellow inhabitants, perhaps in the spirit of Psalm 148, in which the divine choirmaster calls "sun and moon" to praise God, along with "wild animals" and "creeping things," and even the "sea monsters and all deeps" (vv. 3, 7, 10). We should not disturb them while they do their work. Again, so much of our learning to pray involves noticing what God is doing all around us, a matter that we will take up in some greater detail in the next chapter.

For now, we will continue to discuss praying toward the reign of God by returning to our journey through the Triduum—that is, the Holy Thursday, Good Friday, and Easter Vigil observances that stand at the heart of the Christian Year. As we noted in chapter 4, since the Triduum culminates with the baptismal rite of the Easter Vigil, everything that we do in those three days points toward baptism and the mission that we are given in and through it. To this point in our discussion together, we have reflected on the ways that Holy Thursday footwashing and our Good Friday journey to the cross shape us for our baptismal vocation to intercessory work. Now we will do similar reflection on Easter, and in particular, the liturgy for the Easter Vigil. Its readings and its prayers provide a series of windows that reveal God's desires for the world, thereby providing a response to the question posed earlier: What does God want? By grace, we are invited to participate in this work that God is doing, joining it both with the intercessions of our spoken prayers and with the intercessions of our hands and feet.

The Easter Vigil and Its Prayers: A Glimpse of the Reign of God

As with Holy Thursday and Good Friday, Easter is not simply about the wonderful work that God did for Jesus in raising him from the dead. It is about the work of resurrection that God began there and continues to do. A Pauline text often read on Easter Sunday[23] asserts this saving dynamic:

> If for this life only we have hoped in Christ, we are of all people most to be pitied. But in fact Christ has been raised from the dead, the first fruits of those who have died. For since death came through a human being, the resurrection of the dead has also come through a human being; for as all die in Adam, so will all be made alive in Christ. (1 Cor. 15:19-22)

According to another Pauline text that we examined earlier, that work begins in baptism and is shaped by the same, that is, by life within the Baptismal Covenant:

> Do you not know that all of us who have been baptized into Christ Jesus were baptized into his death? Therefore we have been buried with him by baptism into death, so that, just as Christ was raised from the dead by the glory of the Father, so we too might walk in newness of life. (Rom. 6:3-4)

This Romans text is always read at the Easter Vigil[24] (within the context of Rom. 6:3-11), and is one of the keys to understanding its baptismal intent. As we noted in chapter 5, this text calls the baptized to stand under the cross with Jesus, interceding with our spoken and embodied prayers. In like manner, it calls us to pray within the dynamics of the Resurrection, dreaming along with God and then living toward those dreams.

A shape of that dream is presented in the long set of Old Testament passages appointed for use at the vigil.[25] Each of these readings is paired with a collect, a prayer that calls upon God to continue the saving work referenced in the reading. Upon the completion of the Old Testament readings, the Service of the Word concludes with the Romans 6 text and then the empty-tomb narrative appointed for that year.[26] Then follows the Service of the Baptismal Covenant and the Service of the Table. That order suggests that, through baptism, one becomes a participant in this narrative of salvation. The United Methodist Service of the Baptismal Covenant underscores that connection in its opening sentences when it says, "Through the sacrament of baptism we are initiated into Christ's holy Church. We are incorporated into God's mighty acts of salvation."[27]

We will look at three of these Old Testament readings, along with the collects that accompany them: "The Creation" (Gen. 1:1–2:4a); "Israel's Deliverance at the Red Sea" (Exod. 14:10-31; 15:20-21); and "New Life for God's People" (Ezek. 37:1-14). Many consider a reading of the first two, Genesis and Exodus, essential to a proper observance of the Easter Vigil, while the Ezekiel text is a personal favorite. Each passage speaks of what God has done, while each also points forward, toward God's dream for the world, toward

God's ongoing work. Each of them, therefore, serves to shape the church's intercessory mission.

The Creation (Genesis 1:1–2:4a)

Both Genesis Creation narratives (see also Gen. 2:4b-25)[28] provide foundation for the environmental concerns expressed earlier. The Easter Vigil appoints the first narrative (Gen. 1:1–2:4a), so we focus there. This passage invites us to join God in proclaiming the goodness of creation (Gen. 1:31, "very good"). No person who actively participates with God in this way should be able to treat creation as an afterthought or, worse, with disdain. Rather, they will notice all that is around them, and they will intercede on its behalf. The charge to "have dominion over . . . every living thing" (Gen. 1:28) and to have use of "every green plant for food" (1:30) will not be heard as license to exploit, but rather as a call to stewardship. Moreover, it is an invitation to joy and wonder.

But this narrative speaks to more than stewardship of the natural world, as important as that is. The collect calls us to hear it in terms of God's ongoing creative and restorative activity:

> Almighty God, you wonderfully created, yet more wonderfully
> restored,
> the dignity of human nature.
> Grant that we may share the divine life
> of the one who shared our humanity,
> Jesus Christ our Savior. Amen.[29]

This prayer reflects 2 Corinthians 5:17, where Paul insists, "If anyone is in Christ, there is a new creation: everything old has passed away; see, everything has become new!" The assembly of the baptized participates in this ongoing work of the new creation. We come to our prayers asking, What needs to be restored? and How does God want to bring forth something new? Indeed, what does God want?

Consider this in relation to Genesis 1: During the weeks that I was writing this chapter, yet more shootings occurred on and around American college campuses.[30] Because events like these continue occurring, my university has added active shooter drills to our regular round of fire and storm drills. To the extent possible, we must be ready for tornadoes and angry people with high-powered weapons. But what else can believers do? We are, of course, called to prayer.

I have done several prayer walks around our Southern Methodist University campus, both as an individual devotional exercise and in concert with others. For example, in March of 2013 Perkins students Joanne Pounds and Kelly Anderson organized a "Walk and Roll Prayer Service," in which we followed a walking route that was also fully accessible to persons in wheelchairs and scooters, thus the "roll" part of the title.[31] We sang as we walked (or rolled), and we stopped at three locations on campus—Meadows School of the Arts, the Memorial Health Center, and the Edwin L. Cox School of Business. At each place, we read scriptures and offered prayers of thanksgiving and intercession. According to university rules, in order to hold such an outside event we had to gain permissions from our campus police department and from various other entities, including the three places where we prayed. When the organizers visited the police department, they gave the necessary permission while also asking if we were going to come to their station and pray for them. We didn't do that, primarily because we couldn't go that far and arrive back at Perkins by the end of one hour, but we did include them in our closing prayer.

So perhaps we need to do another SMU/Perkins prayer walk, going to different places next time. We might also want to do a prayer walk to intercede against the gun violence that could occur here or elsewhere, but also to lament the violence that has, in fact, occurred in our backyard—the less widely publicized sexual assaults and other violent crimes that occur on our campus and others like it. Whether or not we do another walking service, in our other prayers we can intercede for a cessation of violence and the amelioration of its causes. As we always insist, the prayers of our mouths should lead to the intercessions that we will do with our bodies. Thus do we imagine the new creation, praying our way toward that vision.

Israel's Deliverance at the Red Sea (Exodus 14:10-31; 15:20-21)

The narrative of Israel's deliverance at the Red Sea has been a fountainhead for many dreams of liberation. Hear the text: Although the Egyptian army had cornered Israel at the Red Sea, God's promise stood firm. God interceded, fighting for them against the Egyptians and leading them to freedom. When they realized that they were free, then they danced and sang (Exod. 14:14, 31; 15:20-21). The collect reminds us that we hear this text not simply as a report of what God did, astounding as it was, but as a reminder of God's continuing activity within the church and beyond it. We pray,

> God our Savior, as once you delivered by the power of your mighty arm
> your chosen Israel through the waters of the sea,
> so now deliver your Church and all the peoples of the earth
> from bondage and oppression, to rejoice and serve you in freedom,
> through Jesus Christ our Deliverer. Amen.[32]

The scripture and the prayer draw us toward deeper reflection, wider praying. Who else lives in bondage? We can think of many such persons—victims of the sex trades and those addicted to pornography. We might think of persons bound by poverty, perhaps the victims of usurious payday lenders, and also those who profit from those practices, bound by their greed. We might think of Christians living under persecution and of other Christians, bored and lethargic, who have forgotten that life in the gospel can be a grand adventure. In each case, we can pray for deliverance from bondage to freedom, confident that God will not only effect it, but that God will ask us to participate in that work. There are risks here, but adventure as well. As John Wesley reminded early Methodists, even the Israelites who were told to "stand firm and see the salvation of God" did so by walking . . . on dry ground through the midst of the sea (Exod. 14: 13, 29).[33] As they walked, did they not wonder if the wall of water (14:22) would stay in its place until they reached the other shore? Did they not wonder what awaited them? Again, this narrative is about us as well, and questions like these remain for all those who join the prayer toward liberation and freedom. "Remember your baptism and be thankful."[34]

New Life for God's People (Ezekiel 37:1-14)

Finally, we come to that curious passage from Ezekiel, the vision of the dry bones brought to life by the Spirit of God. I remember a young boy who began to giggle when he heard this text in church for the first time, and it is likely that he heard it better than the rest of us. It presents us with a bizarre image, worthy of the best Halloween ghost stories, with the rattling of bones, their reassembly, and the rebuilding of bodies, beginning with the sinews. Zombies, anyone? Indeed, says the Lord, "can these bones live?" (Ezek. 37:3). According to the text, the Spirit brings the restoration of life, but not without human participation. The mortal one, the prophet, is told to "prophesy to the breath" in the name of God, commanding it to come upon the bones and bring them to life (Ezek. 37:9-10). Why doesn't God just do it? I will never know the answer to that question, but in this biblical narrative, as in so many others like it, the mortals hold a crucial place. Indeed, the story ends without them, and so we pray,

> Eternal God, you raised from the dead our Lord Jesus
> and by your Holy Spirit brought to life your Church.
> Breathe upon us again with your spirit and give new life to your people,
> through the same Jesus Christ our Redeemer. Amen.[35]

That prayer speaks to our own renewal, but *The Book of Common Prayer* (1979) collect for the Ezekiel 37 reading sets its vision toward a wider horizon:

> Almighty God, by the Passover of your Son you have brought us out of sin into righteousness and out of death unto life: Grant to those who are sealed by your Holy Spirit the will and the power to proclaim you to all the world, through Jesus Christ our Lord. Amen.[36]

We should ask, "Where does God want to bring new life and renewal?" and we should follow that by asking, "How can we be part of it?" I think of another experience with this particular text. When my doctors told me in the summer of 2010 that I would soon need heart valve replacement surgery, I was not all that surprised. Steps were becoming harder to climb, and exercise had become more difficult. I would also become short of breath when singing hymns, singing a stanza or two and then dropping out for a few lines. As I have already said, I had the surgery in December 2010. My surgeon did a rebuilding job that a reader of Ezekiel 37 might recognize—open the sternum, artificial valve to cardiac muscle, trim job here, and so on. I entered a cardiac rehabilitation process several weeks after surgery. By the end of January 2011, I had resumed my normal life while my rehabilitation process continued through the end of March. I soon realized that I was much stronger than I had been before the surgery.

Besides taking its normal place within the Easter Vigil that spring, Ezekiel 37:1-14 was appointed as the Old Testament reading for the fifth Sunday of Lent, which fell on April 10, 2011. I heard the text several times that week—in the church that I attend on Sunday mornings, at an evening midweek service in a church where I had gone to make a presentation, and in one of our regular midweek Perkins Chapel services, and thus I was immersed in Ezekiel 37 for the better part of a week. Not long after hearing it those several times, I was singing a hymn in Perkins Chapel when the thought occurred to me: *Have you noticed that now you can now sing without losing your breath?* In fact, I had not noticed until then.

Yes, God restores us in many ways, individually and corporately. Our task is to notice the dry and hopeless places, and then to imagine them in a different state, fully alive and filled with breath. Such imagining will shape our intercessions, both those that we speak in our corporate prayers and those that we enact in our bodies. In ways like this, we enter the dynamic of metanoia in and through our intercessory work, turning from all that destroys life or discourages it, and turning toward the reign of God in its fullness. "Turn, for the reign of God has come near" (Matt. 3:2; 4:17, adapted).

But who does this work of holy imagination? As we established earlier in the book, the vocation to intercede belongs to the entire church by virtue of their baptism, and so it should not be left exclusively to pastors and a few other leaders. Plus, expecting them to do all of this work on their own is an undue burden to place upon them, an invitation to burnout. In the next chapter, we will discuss how a corporate visioning might take shape by using the open-ended discernment question "Why don't we pray for . . . ?"

CHAPTER SEVEN

Intercession and the Discernment of the Christian Community

"Why Don't We Pray For . . . ?"

To this point we have established the connection between baptism and the vocation to intercessory prayer, and we have asked what the contours and themes of the Baptismal Covenant suggest about the shape of those prayers. Since the work of intercession belongs to all baptized Christians, the whole church should participate in them, ideally in a verbal manner. Christians have done this in a variety of ways, through the "Amen," both scripted and spontaneous, through the *kyrie eleison* ("Lord, have mercy"), and with other responses. As we have seen, in some contexts Christians speak their prayers all at once. Sometimes the congregation sings a prayer hymn. Active participation happens in these and a variety of other ways, including the sharing of "joys and concerns" that we see practiced in many congregations.[1] While such participation should occur within public worship, it should also be expressed in the church's ongoing discernment about its public prayers. But how should such discernment be expressed?

The spontaneous sharing of joys and concerns can be a good first step in such a discernment process, but only if it engages the wider obligations expressed in the classic intercessory lists that we discussed in chapter 5. There we learned that Christians are called to pray not only for their own circle of acquaintances, but also for the universal church, for our nation and the whole world, for our local community and its needs, for those who suffer and those in trouble, and for the saints.[2] Pastors, deacons, and other leaders must exercise their teaching office in helping the church comprehend that wider agenda. While teaching it—and the teaching process is never entirely completed—they should also then entrust it to their parishioners' imaginations, believing that the Spirit is at work among them. My question, "Why don't we pray for . . . ?" will help in this task. Note its open-ended structure. As I was developing this baptismal theology for the church's intercessory work, that process began to spark insights in my imagination, including the "Why don't we pray for . . . ?" question and the list that I continue to develop in response to it. Leaders and congregations should discuss questions like this wherever they gather both to pray and to reflect upon their praying.

And so I present "Why don't we pray for . . . ?" as a local church discernment question, much like the "Who's missing?" question that I ask in relation to extending Holy Communion to the unwillingly absent.[3] Questions like these work at the intersection of liturgy and mission, with liturgical work overflowing into mission. As such, they make it difficult for us to decide where liturgy ends and mission begins, and that is the way it should be.[4] The list that I offer here is simply an example of my own brainstorming, and as such it is neither an exhaustive list nor a prescriptive one. As I have presented it in various venues, some have asked me to share my list, and in fact I am sharing some of it here. Most likely, it will be still longer by the time this book is published. But my list is not the primary point; the deeper point is that local churches should do their own discernment, prayerfully developing their own specific lists. Understand, then, that I offer mine as an exercise in holy imagination. Use portions of it if you find them helpful, but more than that, use the list as stimulus for your own imagination. So then, again, why don't we pray for . . . ? At various points along the way, I will share notes as to how I came to think about some of the matters that I name. Each petition sits atop a narrative.

Having given a sampling from my "Why don't we pray for . . . ?" list, I will then reflect upon two examples of corporate discernment that led to deeper community prayer life. I will close the chapter by reflecting upon an excellent example of holy imagination that shaped public prayer, a benediction for a graduation ceremony at Southern Methodist University as developed by Dean William B. Lawrence of Perkins School of Theology.

Why Don't We Pray For . . . ?

So then, why don't we pray for the following?

1. **All of those who are missing**

    Here I am extending the "Who's missing?" question. Living with that question over time may cause us to notice persons in our neighborhood, asking, "Who else is God calling into our fellowship, into our care?" More darkly, this question can evoke thoughts of the many as-yet-unnamed victims of ethnic cleansing and war.

2. **All parents, and especially those raising children with special needs**

3. **Those who struggle to fulfill their vocation as parents, and especially for those who have become disappointed in their children, that they not lose hope in them**

4. **Autistic children, and other children who seem odd and different, that they be protected from violence and other oppression**

5. **The blessing and strengthening of relationships among fathers and sons, mothers and daughters, and among in-laws**

6. **Children of all ages who find themselves estranged from their parents, and the parents who feel a similar estrangement from their children**

    Because of the dynamics of differentiation, tension between parents and children may be inevitable, but sometimes that tension hardens into bitterness and an estrangement that can be difficult to overcome. Whether transitory or permanent, such estrangement is painful.

    This petition came to mind one day as I was reading Psalm 27, verses 9 and 10 in particular: "Do not hide your face from me. Do not turn your servant away in anger, you who have been my help. . . . If my father and mother forsake me, the LORD will take me up." We should join our prayer to that of the psalmist.

7. **Parents of children who have committed crimes, and those whose children and grandchildren are incarcerated**

8. **Prisoners awaiting execution, their families, and their victims**

I thought of this petition when I read a pitiful news story that described thirty-one-year-old Joshua Maxwell sobbing and apologizing as he lay strapped to a gurney in the execution chamber, moments from his death.[5] I think of scenes like this more and more often, in large part because I live in the state that leads the nation in executions. Some posit that the execution of those who have committed murder brings closure to the loved ones of the victim, but I wonder what closure comes with the continuing rehashing of events that occurs during the appeals process and around the time of the execution. Furthermore, as a matter of doctrine, Christians believe that the last propitiatory death has occurred (see Heb. 10:10). For these and many other reasons, I am convinced that Christians should be far more troubled by state-sanctioned executions than we seem to be. Regardless of our political and theological conclusions on the matter, death row and executions represent multiple layers of tragedy and suffering. Should we not pray for all those involved?

9. **Coaches of children's and youth sports teams**

I have long been interested in sports, both as participant and fan, and of late, I have been encouraged to do more theological reflection on these matters, as more churches are conducting youth sports programs like Upward. Actually, this attempt to relate athletics and Christian spirituality extends back at least to the turn of the twentieth century, to the Young Men's Christian Association (YMCA).[6]

How should a youth sports program run by the church be different from Little League and other such programs? Moreover, how should we respond to the growing intensity of youth sports, and at ever-younger ages? How will we know if we fail to include these cultural matters in our intercessory agenda?

Nevertheless, sport is sport, and one can learn from its disciplines and competition. For these coaches, we might pray that they not fear giving appropriate tests and challenges, but that they remain compassionate and realistic about the children and youth under their supervision.

10. Public school teachers

Theirs is difficult work, not always highly valued yet vitally important. And so it is important that we support them. As with the coaches, we should pray that they not fear giving appropriate tests and challenges, while they remain compassionate and realistic about their students' potential.

11. Scholars under tenure review and those who review their work

This one is particularly close to me, having (now) successfully moved through the university promotion process. In many cases, part of one's reward for making that journey is the opportunity to become a reviewer for others. On both ends, the review process is a labor-intensive and potentially stressful experience for individuals and often for their families. Churches in university and college towns would do well to include such petitions in their prayers.

Academia is not the only profession that involves review processes. Churches would do important ministry in praying for those engaged in all levels of such evaluation.

12. Persons "living in the closet," and all of those who care about them, and for all of those who must make adjustments if and when they come out

13. Gay, lesbian, and transgendered persons, that they be protected from violence

14. All who live alone

15. The homeless and the hungry

16. Persons who receive good news and persons who receive bad news, and all who care for them

17. Those facing mastectomies or any serious surgery

18. The environment, the rivers and other waters, the air, and all of God's creatures?

What would a set of intercessions for creation look like? As with much Christian practice, most likely we will figure it out as we go along, constantly refining our understanding and our practice.

19. Refugees in transit, including those leaving Central America and Mexico and traveling across the Chihuahua Desert into Arizona, New Mexico, and Texas

For those who live in the states along the Mexican border, this matter is constantly before us, and, for that matter, it cannot be ignored anywhere in the United States. This petition occurred to me while reading one of our SMU Common Reading project books, *The Devil's Highway*, by Luis Alberto Urrea,[7] which provides an account of the suffering that many of these transients endure.

20. All who commute, that they learn to drive gently, and especially for people forced to sit in traffic jams

Interlude #1: Praying for Persons Stuck in Traffic Jams? Really?

Given some of the more intense issues that I have named thus far, it may seem odd to talk about praying for persons sitting in traffic, that is, until you're the one sitting there crawling along, relatively helpless, with your carefully planned schedule falling apart as you wait. So then, why not make prayers like this one? Indeed, almost every time I pray something like this in church, that we learn to drive gently, I hear a knowing giggle or two, so it appears to touch a nerve. We could, in fact, even develop a prayer office for such occasions.

I first thought of such petitions following conversations with two of my Order of Saint Luke brothers. I had experienced a day during which I sat through no less than three long delays on Route 75 in Dallas. Each was caused by an accident, none of which, thankfully, directly involved me. But they did occur within the community and world that I inhabit, and what affects one affects everyone else. That can become especially true as one's level of irritation increases.

The first traffic jam occurred while I was taking my son to an orthodontist appointment, and the second, on the other side of the highway, as I was driving him back to school. So he was late twice. The third happened later in the day, while I was traveling to a meeting with one of the brothers to discuss aspects of this very book. I showed up for that meeting about thirty minutes late, and I hate being late. Now when I speak of traffic jams, I am not simply talking about typical rush-hour congestion—in the city, one learns to live with that and it becomes an odd part of normal. I'm referring, rather, to the kind of mess that is created when accidents occur in the midst of the normal congestion. That day, I confessed first to the one brother and then to the next, that such traffic jams tend to stress me out, and that I have never dealt with them very well. Each brother, in turn, nodded knowingly and spoke to an experience much like mine. In a calmer moment, then, I thought, *Why not develop a set of intercessions crafted for such an occasion?* And so I did. Such a set might include the following prayer foci:

- For patience, and for an ability to take this seemingly wasted time for prayer
- For a blessing on the life and work of those who may be inconvenienced by our not showing up on time
- For the safety and well-being of those caused pain by accidents that may have occurred
- For emergency personnel, ambulance and tow-truck drivers, firefighters, and police officers
- For all who travel on the highways, including truck drivers and delivery personnel
- For patience for my fellow drivers, that they not displace on others any anger that they may feel as a result of this delay

For obvious reasons, I do not suggest that persons read such prayers while behind the wheel, even if stopped or slowed to a crawl. Rather, they can offer them at other times, and as a result of that praying, hope to recall some or all of them when the inevitable traffic challenges arise at some future point. I have actually managed to remember parts of these petitions on a few such occasions and have found them somewhat helpful, although I still have a long way to go before I reach perfection on this matter. By the way, I pray them with my eyes open.

Now then, back to the task before us. Why don't we pray for the following?

21. Those stuck waiting in airports, and those who fly and maintain airplanes and jets, as well as flight attendants

This petition is an extension of the focus on travel and its challenges. Remember that airports can be high-stress places, and those who manage airports and airlines must work very hard. Watch flight attendants the next time you fly and think about the work that they do. They spend much time on their feet, in the relatively cramped space of the plane's aisle, trying to maintain a both businesslike and cheerful demeanor. That can't be easy.

22. Those who face illness or other difficult needs while traveling far from home

23. Sixteen-year-olds who are learning to drive, parents and other instructors who teach them, and those who share the streets and highways with them

This one occurred to me in the summer during which my youngest son began learning to drive. Some congregations do the laying on of hands with prayer for all new drivers, as their way of reminding them of the responsibility that accompanies their newfound freedom. For the Christian, driving should be seen as an extension of one's discipleship.

24. Those who drive trucks and those persons who teach and mentor them, in thanksgiving for their work, and their safety

When I was six years old, I went through a short period when I was fascinated by trucks and could name and identify many of them by manufacturer's name. Like a long-forgotten language, that knowledge faded about the time that I discovered baseball. Then, my older son trained as a truck driver and began his work. I haven't regained my former knowledge about trucks, but now as I'm driving I notice most of the trucks and try to remember to pray for those who drive them.

25. Engineers and other scientists who work to reduce greenhouse emissions and figure out ways to decrease fuel consumption

This question emerged in conversation with Deacon Dianne B. Salter, who was my colleague at First United Methodist Church, Chambersburg, Pennsylvania, from 1985 to1990. Her husband, Charles, is a retired engineer with Mack Trucks, Inc., who consults with the National Research Council under contract to the Environmental Protection Agency about these issues. We should pray for these and other scientists.

26. Cardiologists, medical technicians, and all of those undergoing cardiac tests and/or surgery

27. Veterinarians and other people who care for animals, both our pets and those who belong to others

Blessing of the animals, often done in or around the Feast Day of Saint Francis of Assisi, October 4, can be a first step in praying for creation. Why not, then, pray in support of those who care for animals? A dentist friend once reminded me that while doctors for human beings must learn one anatomy, veterinarians must learn multiple anatomies. I need to do a better job of noticing them.

28. Dentists and dental hygienists, and those who cannot afford dental care

I thought of this one while in the midst of a routine exam and cleaning. The dental hygienist said to me, "People never want to see us."

29. Those who do medical research, that they work diligently and with integrity

For a cautionary word that echoes within this petition, read the book by Rebecca Skloot, *The Immortal Life of Henrietta Lacks* (New York: Crown, 2010). Cancer cells originally cultured from Henrietta Lacks remain an important tool in much significant cancer and other medical research. But neither she nor her family were consulted or asked permission regarding their use.[8]

30. District attorneys and officers of the court, and especially those in danger of retaliation from those whom they have prosecuted

This one occurred to me after three murders occurred in Kauffman County, Texas, in fall 2012—an assistant district attorney, the district attorney, and his wife. When the murders occurred, some darkly thought it the work of white supremacist gangs. It was, rather, the work of a disgruntled former justice of the peace.[9]

31. Financial planners and development officers for universities, other schools, and charitable organizations; and people with wealth

I thought of this petition while listening to the sermon "A Fool and His Money," delivered by the Reverend Jeff Hall of Cox Chapel, Highland Park United Methodist Church, Dallas, Texas, on August 1, 2010. The sermon was based on Luke 12:13-21, a text commonly named the "Parable of the Rich Fool."

32. Those who manage our water supplies

33. Public school music and art teachers, and their departments, as they are often forced to work with fewer and fewer resources

34. Sanitation workers, electricians, and plumbers

35. Ranchers and farmers, and especially those who must work on Sundays

This one came to me in a conversation held at First United Methodist Church, Henrietta, Texas, located in the midst of Texas ranching country, on October 7, 2012. I was discussing extended table and my "Who's missing?" question. When I mentioned nurses and others who must work on Sundays, someone said, "I have a new one for you—ranchers and cowboys." Of course, "Who's missing"" and "Why don't we pray for . . . ?" are closely related questions, and each is about noticing the other.

36. Persons who must work outside in extreme heat or cold

Again, we are called to notice the other, and through such prayerful noticing, God deepens our compassion.

37. "Those who stand all day in warehouses and factories"[10]

I am directly borrowing this one from Joyce Rupp, a member of the Servite Community, whose book *Walk in a Relaxed Manner: Life Lessons from the Camino,* reflects on the pilgrimage that she and Father Tom Pfeffer made on the ancient Camino de Santiago. Each day as they began walking, they prayed for the grace to notice their fellow pilgrims and others whom they encountered. As they were concluding their morning prayers one day, they walked past a large open warehouse, and this petition emerged in them. Reading Rupp's story brought me to memories of my own summer job experience in a factory warehouse, and especially to memories of how my feet felt toward the end of that summer. They hurt, in part because I had not invested in the right kind of boots. Of course, most persons who work in such places don't have the opportunity to return to school at the end of the summer, and for some, buying new boots at the right time may present a challenge.

38. Migrant farmworkers, their children, and their schools

39. Undocumented workers and those who employ them

While discussing "Why don't we pray for . . . ?" during a presentation at the August 2011 NAAC Conference referenced earlier, I mentioned the need to pray for undocumented workers, and I noted one conundrum among many—that the North Texas economy likely depends on their work. Having said that, someone added "and those who employ them" to my petition. And so, the conversation deepens and expands, as does the church's prayer.

40. Persons who suffer exhaustion from working too hard, for too long, including pastors and church leaders suffering from burnout, and those who long to work but cannot find the opportunity

41. Photographers, that they may see and notice more things, thereby helping us to see and notice more completely

Interlude #2: Praying for All of the People a University Comprises . . . and Your Neighborhood Too

This last petition emerged from a somewhat longer narrative. As you can see in the preceding section and at various points throughout this book, I am convinced that it is important to notice the daily work that people do. Such prayer can deepen our compassion for others, and I believe that can help persons perceive their daily work as an extension of their discipleship, thus changing both them and the work. I offered my prayer for photographers within the prayers of the people during a Perkins Chapel service that included the baptism of our university photographer, Hillsman Jackson. He is a man with a particular gift for noticing the world through a camera lens. And so I prayed "for photographers, that they may see and notice more things, thereby helping us to see and notice more completely."

That I was able to frame the petition in this way resulted from the direct influence of another artist, Professor Eileen D. Crowley, Associate Professor of Liturgy and Worship Arts at the Catholic Theological Union of Chicago. Dr. Crowley is my colleague in the Christian Initiation Seminar at the North American Academy of Liturgy, and through a presentation she made to us in January 2013, I had come to see the camera as a particularly postmodern way of noticing things. As she asserted, "Everyone with a smart phone is now carrying around both a camera and a movie camera," and many use those tools to post images to Facebook and other social media. She shared about her website, "Our Callings in the World,"[11] and had encouraged students and others to post photographs, videos, and written narratives that witness to their understanding of Christian vocation. I recommend it.

I adapted her insight about smart phones for a practicum exercise that I conduct within our Introduction to Christian Worship course. I remind my students of my "Why don't we pray for . . . ?" question, and then, with due credit given to Dr. Crowley, ask them to take one photograph that expresses a possible response to that question. Specifically, I tell them,"There's no right or wrong here, so let your prayerful imagination roam free. Let the searching for the photograph itself be an act of prayer. Print the photograph, and bring it to your practicum session, along with one or two sentences that express how you would pray with, for, and/or about what you see in the photograph."

My students do the assignment, and seemingly with some enthusiasm. My favorite student photo to date has been one depicting a polar bear, which I guarantee was not taken on our campus. SMU has an active feral cat population, and thus fewer mice, but no polar bears. As my student insisted, however, we should pray for the polar bears, and for all of God's creatures. I wouldn't argue.[12]

With and without my camera in hand, I aspire to notice more, to gather more persons and things into my thanksgivings and intercessions, including photographers themselves. My Perkins colleague Alyce M. McKenzie commends a similar watchfulness, which she calls a "knack for noticing," deeming it essential to both the preacher's and the writer's crafts. She insists that the preacher should never leave home without a notebook or some means of recording thoughts and insights, lest a helpful one be lost. One can extend her insight to praying for our neighborhoods and for the world.[13]

I am convinced that imagination begets more imagination, and thus sometimes it comes in a sudden burst. For example, the following list occurred in the midst of the Pre-Advent Quiet Day that our Perkins Order of Saint Luke chapter held in late November 2012. I sat in front of Perkins Chapel, with our Bridwell Library in view and our Meadows School of the Arts just around the corner, watching the SMU grounds crew planting winter flowers. Various participants of our campus were walking past. In the space of about fifteen minutes, I wrote the following in my journal: "Why don't we pray for . . ."

- Arborists
- Librarians
- The SMU grounds crew
- Engineers and the school of engineering
- Those living in dormitories

- Undergraduates, and those trying to find places on campus (travelers, neighbors) (While I was sitting there writing, a seemingly befuddled and exasperated young man walked up to me and asked, "Could you tell me where Perkins Administration Building is?" I told him where it is located—that it was back in the direction from which he had just come—to which he replied, "But, I was just there.")
- Our campus neighbors
- All who create beauty . . . musicians, architects, sculptors who work with metal
- Those trying to find money to go to school
- Our university and school benefactors
- Dancers
- Actors
- Fitness coaches
- Those who are ambitious, that they may relax and know that they're loved
- The anxious

As I wrote my list, it became prayer. Try this exercise in your own neighborhoods. Take a leisurely walk, with camera or notebook in hand, and notice things. Then let your noticing be shaped into thanksgivings and intercessions.

Once again, back to our project. Why don't we pray for . . .

42. College and university students who must take classes and write papers and exams in a language other than their native language

Navigating college and graduate school is challenging enough on a number of levels. Those who choose to do it outside of their first language and culture face even greater challenges.

43. Muslims observing Ramadan, and Jews observing High Holy Days

44. Couples engaged to be married, and married couples as an act of renewal

Noting the wider range of church ceremonies that once surrounded marriage—betrothal rites and house blessing among them—Kenneth Stevenson has suggested praying for recently engaged couples, perhaps in a rite including the laying on of hands.[14]

45. Couples who are contemplating divorce, those who care about them, and those for whom they care

46. Foster parents and children who live in foster care

47. Parents who don't know where their adult children are living or what they are doing

Relatively brief gaps in knowledge may occur because persons are simply busy or preoccupied, or perhaps someone finds himself or herself in a bit of a snit. There are, however, parents for whom the absence of even basic information about their children has stretched to years. Sometimes it is the result of a deep alienation, but there may be other causes, such as abduction or war.

48. Persons who must care both for their children and for older adults

49. Elderly persons who are downsizing, and all those who are moving from their homes and their families

50. Teenagers in their encounter with the Holy, and that they be able to experience more joy than sorrow

During one of the long silences practiced during the three daily services at Taizé—sometimes they last as long as ten minutes—a group of teenagers seated not far away from me began giggling, and with varying results they struggled to stifle it. Initially, it was irritating, but then I began to get over it, remembering similar times in retreat services while I was that age. One might understand the giggling as a nervous reaction in the face of the numinous. Or perhaps something really funny happened at the wrong time and they'll have a good story to tell at a future reunion.

51. Children and youth on school breaks and summer vacations, that they may use their time to good purpose

52. People living with Alzheimer's disease and other forms of dementia, and those who love them and care for them

53. People who have blessed us in the past, with whom we no longer have contact, and perhaps have largely forgotten

One doesn't have to be living with dementia to forget people and things. With my various moves related to churches and schools, I have had the opportunity to meet (and, unfortunately, forget) many people. Given the transient nature of contemporary life, mine is not a unique experience. But remember, God never forgets. That is both a gift to us and our hope. For whatever reason, occasionally one of these long-forgotten persons comes to mind, and more often than not, the memory is a blessing. Hopefully my remembering blesses them as well, and perhaps more so if I remember to give thanks for them and pray for them.

54. Victims of sexual predators, especially when the predators have been clergy or church workers

We should not, in most cases, pray for such persons publicly by name. But offering a general petition may encourage those who are suffering, and perhaps will lead toward the repentance of predators.

55. Church members with celiac disease, their pastors and congregations, as they seek ways to serve and receive Holy Communion in both the bread and the wine (As before, "Who's missing?")

56. Those living with mental illness, and those who care for them

57. Those who live with depression, and perhaps especially around the Christmas holidays

Depression is a scourge to many and also a killer, and so we should remember such persons throughout the year. In most cases, we should not publicly pray for depressed persons by name. Some churches conduct "Blue Christmas" or "Longest Night" services for persons who become more aware of their struggle in and around the holidays. Holding a special service for them may offer some advantages, but for a variety of reasons, we should consider offering this petition within the full Sunday assembly. Shall we, indeed, bear one another's burdens, and thus fulfill the law of Christ (Gal. 6:2)?

58. Those struggling with addiction

59. Those without effective access to health care

60. Women who have suffered miscarriages, even in the early weeks of pregnancy when perhaps they were the only ones who knew

This petition emerged in a conversation that occurred after I made a presentation on "Why don't we pray for . . . ?" to a North Texas Annual Conference meeting for persons in process toward ordination.

61. Victims of robbery, and also those who have stolen from them

62. Those caught in the cycles of gang life and gang warfare

I have now shared part of my list, which, as I said earlier, continues to grow. I could share more, but that is not the point, and even now you may sense that I have begun to repeat myself, or that I am missing important themes and foci. Hopefully, my response to the question, "Why don't we pray for . . . ?" has sparked your own thinking. You may find yourself in disagreement with some of the ways that I have framed my responses. If so, that is a good thing. My particular list is not the point, and any one person's list will always be limited. Furthermore, if we were to have such a conversation in a church worship planning group, what I present here would not be a finished discussion but only my contribution. I believe that I am stretched by my encounters with the gospel, with the world and its people, and that through the grace of God my understanding and compassion are expanding. Nevertheless, I can never be more than a particular person with particular perspectives. In spite of my best intentions and aspirations, my "Why don't we pray for . . . ?" list is going to reflect what I think about and talk about, where I work, and whom I know. My goal is that you and your church learn to live with this question and that you respond to it together. This entire dialogue, of course, is based on the foundational insight that the vocation to prayer is rooted in baptism, and thus it belongs to the whole church. I will turn now to two accounts of churches who practiced such discernment, one quite intentionally, and the other somewhat on the spur of the moment.

"Why Don't We Pray For . . . ?" Stories from Two Churches

A Prayer Group at St. Matthew's United Methodist Church, Houston, Texas

The Wednesday evening prayer meeting at St. Matthew's United Methodist Church in Houston had been in place for several years when I visited with several of their members on a Sunday afternoon in January 2012. Their pastor, the Reverend Frank Coats, was a student of mine at Perkins. He is also my brother within the Order of Saint Luke, and we remain in conversation on various matters. Having heard my presentations and effectively led my set of "Prayers in an Anti-Docetic Mode" at the 2011 Order of Saint Luke Retreat (see chapter 5), he is well aware of the arguments that I present in this book, and they have had some influence on his practice. For example, he has led a version of the anti-docetic intercessions at St. Matthew's, adding several insightful biddings, including these:

- Those who send others into war
- Those who work nights
- All teachers, administrators, and all who work under increasing pressure

As he described it to me, their Wednesday night gatherings began with singing, followed by scripture reading and his comments on it. Then they engaged in free prayer, followed by spoken prayers in response to the biddings listed within the United Methodist "An Order for Evening Prayer and Praise."[15] Here they were using the classic prayer list that we discussed earlier. By many indications, then, their gathering was well on its way toward being a thoughtful and effective prayer group well before they met me. They were accustomed to praying together, for their church and neighborhood, and for the world.

When I met with them, I gave them a brief overview of my work and thought, and then when I arrived at the "Why don't we pray for . . . ?" question, they responded readily and with insight. Again, their formation had prepared them well. A Houston-area pizza-delivery man had been robbed recently, so one man suggested that we pray for persons who make deliveries, as well as taxi drivers. Another suggested that we pray for church administrators. I described my experience of driving past the Texas State Penitentiary while en route to Houston. I shared about seeing the many cars in the parking lot, which led me to prayers for the guards, the prisoners, and their families. Someone followed that testimony by saying that we should pray for criminals and victims of crime, and another insisted that we should pray for oppressors and terrorists.

Moving on from that topic, another said that we should pray for children leaving home to go away to school and enter adult life. A member of the prayer group who serves as a volunteer custodian on Sundays shared a story from a time when he was cleaning and he heard someone break the window of his truck. Now he prays for the neighborhood as he walks the grounds and picks up trash. A former missionary to Africa spoke of the need to move deeper into prayer by "learning a different people," that is, by becoming acquainted with another culture. She insisted that they could do that right within their own city, and indeed, many of us could do the same where we live.

And thus many conversations develop when those who acknowledge their vocation to prayer are encouraged to brainstorm together in the Spirit.[16]

Prayers for Japan? A Discernment of the Assembly, Occurring in the Moment

Sometimes the process is not as deliberate as what we saw at St. Matthew's, but even then we should assume that the Spirit is at work among the baptized. Here is a story of a decisive and bold discernment that occurred on a Sunday morning in the middle of a worship service. My student William Eason related this during a classroom sermon on the parable of the wheat and the weeds (Matt. 13:24-30, 36-43). He delivered the sermon within weeks of the tsunami that struck Japan in March 2011. With his permission, I share a portion of it here:

> Jesus makes clear that we are to focus not on the weeds, but on planting, nurturing, encouraging and growing the gospel wheat, the children

> of God. Rather than pulling up the weeds, Jesus encourages us to be strong, bountiful gospel wheat.
>
> Over the past two weeks, we have watched in horror as one of the largest earthquakes in recorded history shook Japan. As if that were not enough, a tsunami came rushing in. We watched on YouTube as waves destroyed homes. We now watch as nuclear plants fail; devastation seems certain. It is in the wake of this horror that an enemy, a prowler, comes into the precious garden, among the wheat and the weeds. The prowler is racism. In my local congregation, I have several men who are veterans of World War II. These men have painful memories of past events, painful memories that have shaped their response to this growing devastation. One of these men has even teased me quite ferociously from time to time because I drive a Japanese car. As the congregation gathered and concerns for prayer were offered, the congregation was asked to pray for those in Japan.
>
> Some people gasped. After all, we don't bring up this kind of topic in front of these men. I saw the look of shock on their faces, perhaps even anger. . . . It was then that he stood, a man who was as rigid as stone, an officer who had spent years in World War II in the Pacific. The congregation fell silent; what would he say? He stood, and said unwaveringly: "I want to be the one to pray for those who are suffering in Japan. Innocent people are suffering and they are no different than me. We are all children of God."
>
> In that moment I realized what Jesus was communicating in this parable.[17]

One bold disciple asserted not so much his military rank as his standing among the children of God, and so the community decided to pray for Japan. Given this story, in addition to asking the "Why don't we pray for . . . ?" question, you might ask if there is anything for which your church cannot pray, and if so, why is that the case? What good will happen when such taboos are finally set aside?

In the final section of this chapter, we will look at a prayer that Dean William B. Lawrence of Perkins School of Theology delivered in the context of our Southern Methodist University commencement exercises. While such praying is not forbidden in the context of a private university such as ours, one might not expect to find prayer of this depth at a graduation ceremony, especially given the wide range of religious backgrounds present there, including many persons who do not adhere to any religious tradition.

Holy Imagination at Work: Dean William B. Lawrence's Benediction, Southern Methodist University Commencement

Dean Lawrence's prayer provides us with a strong example of holy imagination at work. While not prayers of the people in the strictest sense, this benediction prays for the university, its faculty and graduates, in deep ways. Here is the text of the prayer as he offered it at the May 12, 2012, SMU graduation:

Now may the One whose Word preceded every beginning
  And will abide after every ending
  Be with us to bless us on this day
    When so much is coming to a close
    And so much more is just about to commence.
Accept the blessings of God, who prompts us to great joy,
  As we celebrate the success that so many have achieved
  And smile at the failures that have been so graciously forgiven.
Accept the blessings of God who prompts us to deep sorrow
  For those who began the journey with us
    and are concluding it elsewhere,
  For those who began the journey with us
    and are still without a conclusion,
  For those who began the journey with us
    and whose time on earth ended before their education could.
Accept the blessings of God who prompts us to weep

In tears of gratitude for teachers who believed in us when we doubted ourselves
In tears of thanks for siblings and spouses and sons and daughters who celebrate with us
though they do not understand
what we study
or why
And in tears of respect for parents
who sacrificed more than even love could require
who labored so we might learn
who kept vigil so we could rest
who maintained hope so that we would be free from our doubts.
Accept the blessings of God who prompts us to keep our minds and hearts open
So that we can learn about arrogance without being arrogant about learning
So that we can long for peace without feeling that war is the only way to win it
So that we can labor for success without needing others to fail for us to gain it
And accept the belief that, on this day, the light of learning that informs our minds
Will also infuse our souls
And transform our ways
Then those of us who have studied law
Will establish justice
And those of us who have studied business
Will practice equity
And those of us who have studied science
Will embrace mystery
And those of us who have studied art
Will create energy
And all of us who have been committed to study

Will renew our commitment to serve
Until every one of the children in God's world
Who feels forced to travel in any manner of darkness
Will journey safely and peacefully
Into great light
AMEN[18]

This prayer emerged in the manner of most good intercessory work, from deep dialogue with the gospel and from compassionate and attentive engagement with his context. William Lawrence developed this form in response to a relatively standard request to offer the benediction at university commencement exercises coupled with his desire to do something more. As he told me, he wanted to do something "that moves beyond the somewhat trite and commonplace connection between graduation and commencement."[19] Rather than speaking generally of endings and beginnings, he pushed himself to be more specific, asking, "What's ending?" And so he thought of classes, relationships, and even careers. He paid attention, beginning with his own narrative.

He remembered a young man with whom he had matriculated many years earlier as an undergraduate at Duke University. During their first semester there, this person had attempted to win a spot on the basketball team. He tried a dunk during open tryouts, hurt his hand, and basically crashed as a student. After the freshman composition final exam, he told his fellow freshman, "I think I just flunked out." And indeed, that is exactly what happened. In framing the prayer, Lawrence said, "I thought of people like him." And he thought of others as well.

He remembered a story that he heard about during his days on the faculty at Duke Divinity School. A committee from the graduating class at North Carolina State University had been assigned the task of nominating a commencement speaker. They searched for common ground and found that they all had watched *Mr. Rogers' Neighborhood* as children, and this commonality held across class and race lines. So Fred Rogers was invited to speak. In his speech, he began by asking his audience to observe one minute of silence, saying to them, "I want you to think of people who helped you get to this day." Relating the story he had heard, Dean Lawrence said, "For the first fifteen seconds, one heard shuffling and some nervous giggling. . . . Then at thirty seconds, it was profoundly silent. . . . At forty-five seconds, one could hear sobbing." In writing his benediction for SMU, Lawrence said, "I kept that moment in mind."[20]

Then, he told me, he turned his imagination to the specific words of the prayer, playing with them. This led him to pair law with justice, business with equity, art with energy, and so on.[21] Here he moved beyond the necessary and valuable work of noticing his surroundings—we work in a university that houses a law school, a business school, and a school of the arts, among others—to imagining what those schools might become in a fuller expression of God's reign. Here we see the spiritual dynamic of metanoia, praying toward the reign of God, which we discussed in chapter 6. Imaginative engagement with his community was turned outward in blessing and intercession.

Note that Lawrence did not develop this prayer hastily, but rather that he thought about it at some length, engaging in a composition process that was prayer itself. Further, he has been offering versions of this prayer over the past decade, so it has been praying within him for some time, shaping both him and others. While this prayer was composed by an individual on behalf of a community, such work also can also be done together by the church and its members as they ask questions like "Why don't we pray for . . . ?," and, as we dare to imagine it, "What does God want?" Those who ask such questions, whether working individually or in groups, are living somewhere between the Spirit's intercession with "sighs too deep for words" (Rom. 8: 26) and Paul's exhortation to "pray without ceasing" (1 Thess. 5:17).

But what good does such praying do? What difference does it make? Quite intentionally, I have left this discussion for the end of the book, and will turn to it in the final chapter. But Dean Lawrence's reflection may offer us a first step in that direction. I asked him about responses to his benediction, including those from SMU colleagues. Over the years he has received numerous requests for copies of the prayer, from both colleagues and visitors, including some nonreligious colleagues, even some who self-identify as atheists. Part of the appeal, he concluded, is that the prayer takes their academic work seriously. He noted, however, that something deeper might be occurring. It seems to touch them, he said, "in places that they're sometimes not ready to admit are there."[22]

CHAPTER EIGHT

So Then, What Difference Does It Make?

Toward Some Positive Assertions

We return now to a question that we asked in the first chapter: Why pray at all? What good does it do? Specifically, what is gained by praying in the ways that we have discussed in this book? Asking "What good does it do?" at this point reflects a theological method followed by many liturgical scholars and theologians. They look to practice and discern meanings from the midst of that very practice. Praying together will teach us something of what praying means and what it accomplishes, and the learning will continue along with our growth in grace. The story of the graduation benediction (chapter 7) offers one suggestion—prayer seems to touch some people "in places that they're sometimes not ready to admit are there."[1] That is another way of saying that God is at work in the midst of it.

So then, we learn what praying means as we pray, and perhaps only in that way. I will admit such a theological method is imprecise, and some might even call it messy.

Naming Some Problems

Praying in Public: Risky, Even a Bit Messy

Praying in public can be risky, and especially when it moves beyond vague generalities. When leaders shape prayers, they must say something specific, thus putting their theological ethical commitments on public display. Furthermore, when free prayers are done, we cannot control what people say. Experienced leaders can point to occasions when prayers became a vehicle for the sharing of detailed information about a person's illness or when dueling prayer intentions emerged around a political issue. Imagine one person praying for the protection of an abortion clinic with another in the same congregation praying for its immediate closing. What happens then, and especially if such patterns persist? One could hardly ignore it.[2] If nothing else, we can see that leading public prayers is not for the faint of heart. Whatever is done, nonanxious leadership is helpful, rooted in the conviction that the church is moving toward perfection but has not yet arrived there. We are learning to pray, and that will always be the case.

Wish Lists for God?

Others will argue that asking God for anything is theologically problematic. Do we imagine God as some manner of cosmic vending machine, almost like an omnipotent magician who will simply intervene in response to our requests?[3] What happens when the desired intervention does not occur? Others will speak negatively about the problems of simply giving our "wish list" to God. Do we not, after all, believe in an all-knowing and ever-present God? If we believe in such a God, then why must we ask? The problem grows worse if we have problems believing in God at all. Consider this reaction from an itinerant professional basketball player upon receiving an invitation to join a team prayer group:

> My response to the prayer circle invitation was a quick lift of the eyebrow and a "Huh, that's interesting," which was a far cry from what I wanted to say, which was, *You've got to be . . . kidding me. You're going to*

> *gather a group of grown men in a hotel room and pray together? Seriously, did no one laugh when you first suggested this?*[4]

Here we have fundamental questions about intercessory prayer itself. Is the practice inherently childish—something that grown men (and women) should be embarrassed to do—at the least, not a fully mature manner of prayer? Such is not an uncommon view, one held by some otherwise-committed Christians who are troubled by some of the theological implications of intercessory prayer. What does one do with such a criticism? It is hard to know, although defining what one wants and needs can be an indication of maturity. We do well, however, to admit that some prayers are, in fact, selfish and childish. Prayers for the increase of one's personal wealth are likely selfish ones, as are prayers for rain when we are unwilling to change our water-use habits (chapter 6). On the other hand, prayers for persons living in poverty and drought conditions are likely not childish prayers, especially if we are also willing to intercede for them in other embodied ways. So then, prayers should be evaluated on a case-by-case basis, as it were, petition by petition. A particular prayer is childish and selfish only if it is, in fact, childish and selfish; and such matters are properly discerned within communities of disciples who are still learning to pray. As in other matters of spiritual growth, however, we should give one another some benefit of the doubt before rushing to judgment.

God Is Present . . . Here, There, Everywhere?

Questions as to where and how God is at work in our praying are not unlike some of the questions that emerge around the Eucharist. Looking to these eucharistic questions can provide us with insight for our consideration of intercessory prayer. How do we understand God's presence in the Eucharist in relation to God's presence in all of creation? Affirming Christ's presence in the breaking of the bread (Luke 24:28-35) does not contradict assertions about God's omnipresence; and indeed, the first claim sheds light on the second. When we are shaped by participation in the Lord's Supper, it also helps us to perceive God's presence in places beyond the eucharistic assembly, in household meals and in the feeding of the hungry, in the fields and vineyards where grain and grapes are grown and harvested, and in kitchens where bread is baked, not to mention in wineries. Discussing God's activity in sacrament and prayer brings us face-to-face with the scandal of particularity.

Philosophically, we affirm that God is present everywhere, in all places and times, and who would argue against this claim? Nevertheless, in the biblical narrative, we are constantly dealing with claims of particularity. God appeared to Abram at a particular time and place, making specific demands and promises: "Go from your country . . . to the land that I will show you. I will make of you a great nation" (Gen. 12:1-2). Why him? Why then and there? God appeared to Moses in a burning bush that was not consumed, and sent him to Pharaoh to bring the Israelites out of Egypt (Exod. 3:1-12). Why a bush in the wilderness? Why him? Both Abram and Moses were far from perfect.

According to scripture, "in Christ God was reconciling the world to himself, not counting their trespasses against them, and entrusting the message of reconciliation to us" (2 Cor. 5:19). As noted, Christ called disciples to participate in his mission, entrusting them with the work of preaching the gospel to the ends of the earth (Acts 1:8; Matt. 28:19-20). We know some of these servants and their foibles, and some have been better witnesses than others. They are . . . us. Thus it is in the biblical narrative and in our ongoing sacramental experience of the means of grace, both in the Eucharist and within the intercessory work that flows from our baptism. God appoints means of grace, calling people to participate in them, in essence promising to show up in particular places. One may wish to argue with the wisdom and justice of these ways, but the biblical narrative insists that this is how God works. And so we pray, odd practice that it may seem to be, especially given some of our less than exemplary petitions. But it appears that God bears with us in spite of ourselves. It can be scandalous, because we are still figuring out how to do it.

This way is wiser, however, than we might at first concede. This claim that God appears in specific places and works in and through specific prayers stands in opposition to the ever-present temptation to a disembodied spirituality, such as the Docetism that we discussed in chapter 5. A God whom we perceive as everywhere can seem benign and indifferent, as one with little regard for the oppressed and those who suffer. On the other hand, the God who frees the Israelites from slavery, who feeds the hungry crowds and heals the suffering, is a God who shows up in particular times and places. It is to this God that we pray, "Please show up and deliver those who suffer." In the end, of course, Christians pray because we are commanded to do so, and because praying is what we do, but it would be hard to maintain the practice simply as a matter of mere obedience. In the spirit of our particular and admittedly strange biblical narrative, I will assert that God is at work in our prayers, doing positive work that might not occur if we failed to pray. We can say the same about our preaching and the rest of our Christian witness. If preachers do not preach, then some persons may not hear the gospel. Such an assertion should, in fact, raise questions about what is lost when we fail to pray, but such knowledge is not available to us. Better to do our assigned work and not have to ask about its neglect. For now, we will presume our willing participation in God's work, which makes us insiders on the question before us: "What difference does all such praying make?" I will address that question with three relatively modest assertions, followed by a fourth, one that is more open-ended in nature.

What Difference Does It Make? Three Assertions

Assertion #1: Our Praying Contributes to Our Sanctification

That is, our praying contributes to our ongoing growth in love. Our baptismal vocation to prayer calls us to open our eyes with compassion, noticing our church and other churches, our community, nation, and the wider world, those in need, as well as creation and all of the living things within it. In doing so, we are drawn beyond ourselves, toward a self-emptying that reflects the mind of Christ and participates in the same. As Paul wrote,

> Let the same mind be in you that was in Christ Jesus,
> who, though he was in the form of God,
> did not regard equality with God

as something to be exploited,
but emptied himself,
taking the form of a slave,
being born in human likeness.
And being found in human form,
he humbled himself,
and became obedient to the point of death—
even death on a cross. (Phil. 2:5-8)

This is God's call to us as well as God's gift. God saves us from ourselves as the Spirit draws us toward a fuller experience of love.

We have seen this spiritual dynamic at work in some of the places that I have described. We heard about it in the story of the Sisters of the Precious Blood, who became aware of the suffering and violence in and around Dayton. They said, "Someone ought to do something," and then they went to pray in the streets, in the very neighborhoods where violence occurred (see introduction and chapter 5). They were already deeply committed to Christ and his mission, but then they moved further into it, and many have joined them. We saw this dynamic at work in my students who insisted on praying for me when I needed it the most, and in the story of the women who rise at night to pray for those in need (chapter 3). One's ability to notice the pain and struggles of others, as well as their aspirations, grows when one responds to such nudges from the Holy Spirit. A deeper awareness of others becomes part of one's character and thus the amount of hospitality in the world increases, even if by a small amount. But, as Charles Wesley suggested, many drops eventually make an ocean.[5]

In a similar fashion, our prayers under the cross, with the crucified Jesus, help us notice and name the suffering around us, on the way to encountering the Risen One who triumphs over that same suffering (chapter 5). Our turning in prayer toward the reign of God helps us to dream of a more just world, both for ourselves and, more importantly, for others (chapter 6). Living with the question "Why don't we pray for . . . ?" is primarily an exercise in noticing what is going on around us. As we pray for veterinarians and plumbers, for victims of abuse and for cardiac patients, we are drawn more deeply into their lives. Our love and compassion for them and others increases, and compassion begets compassion. We experience the dynamic of the Gospels as we thus turn away from our preoccupations and move toward the life God intended for us. As Jesus said to his disciples, "If any want to become my followers, let them deny themselves and take up their cross daily and follow me. For those who want to save their life will lose it, and those who lose their life for my sake will save it" (Luke 9:23-24). This dynamic is experienced by individuals, and by the church as a whole.

As I have said before, the Order of Saint Luke is an important community of prayer for me, particularly our Perkins School of Theology chapter. Given the transient nature of student populations, the chapter is more active in some years than in others. The 2007–2008 school year was an especially good one for us, with strong attendance at both our weekly Morning Prayer and Evening Prayer services. I was glad for that because my father died in October 2007, a victim of esophageal cancer, and little more than a week before he died I found myself in the hospital with what my doctor called "a spectacular pneumonia," perhaps a harbinger of the heart surgery that was to come for me. In his sermon delivered at our May 2008 chapter profession service, our prior, Brother Scot Bontrager, remarked on the way each of us had characteristically borne particular intercessory burdens when we were asked to pray for those in need:

> Something very strange happens when a group of people prays together a lot. You can learn quite a bit about people from what they pray about—without even knowing what you are learning. When thinking about what I was going to say tonight, I realized I know things about some of you that I'm not sure I know how to put into words. Having prayed several times a week with many of you, some of you for three years now, little things start to surface. Br. Mark usually prays for those undergoing cancer treatment. This past year his father died. When I heard it was from cancer, I instantly knew why he had prayed the way he had for so long. And yet, he continues to pray the same prayers. Sr.

> Celia quite often prays for her grandmother . . . Brother A.J. makes sure that we pray for the troubled nations in Africa. What becomes really powerful is when one of us is missing and the rest of us fill in for them. When Br. Mark was out with pneumonia we continued to pray for those undergoing cancer treatments. If Brother A.J. happened to miss a day, we continued to pray for Zimbabwe and Darfur. Individual prayers, when prayed corporately, become corporate prayers. Praying together changes you.[6]

We are, indeed, shaped in positive ways by what we notice, by praying together, and by the communities with whom we pray, and that formation is a discernible fruit of our intercessory work. But God's work never happens simply within ourselves, and thus we move to my second assertion about the effects of our praying.

Assertion #2: Through Our Prayers, God Works to Heal and Bless Others

God is at work in our prayers both to heal and to bless others, and the reach of that blessing is global. In making this assertion, one enters perilous waters theologically. I am not saying that prayers made with the right words in the correct amount of faith—whatever that might be—will always yield the results that we seek. Such an understanding would, indeed, be a magical one, with our prayers serving as the incantations. Such an understanding is absurd at best, and at worst cruel, because it casts those who do not receive what they seek as lacking in faith or perhaps as hiding some secret sin. I can think of parents who have lost children to illness who would have given almost anything to increase their faith, were that possible, or who would have repented of an alleged secret sin, if only they had known what it was. Because of such misguided understandings, "some seriously compassionate Christians end up despairing of intercessory prayer altogether," or if their role in the church forces them to do so, then "in bland and non-specific ways."[7] On the one hand, then, it can be theologically risky to assert God's activity in and through our prayers. On the other hand, however, saying that God really does nothing effective through our praying ends up in a functional atheism, in which intercessions will seem little less than absurd.

I will long remember one of the first healing services that I led. I made it clear, as I still do, that the only promise I would make was the relatively modest pledge to gather and pray for people, in response to the charge expressed in James 5:13-15:

> Are any among you suffering? They should pray. Are any cheerful? They should sing songs of praise. Are any among you sick? They should call for the elders of the church and have them pray over them, anointing them with oil in the name of the Lord. The prayer of faith will save the sick, and the Lord will raise them up; and anyone who has committed sins will be forgiven.

As to theological and personal modesty, I like to place two persons on each prayer team, in part because of the touching that is part of the rite, but even more to move the spotlight away from any one individual's gifts. God is the healer, not us. Given my disclaimers, I received a surprise on the following Sunday when one of those who had come for prayer said, "The ringing in my ears has stopped," and he attributed the change to the prayers we had offered. I was surprised, but why? Our prayers do not force God to act, and only God knows how a particular prayer has been answered, but if God is God, then we should not be surprised when we receive what we pray for. God is at work. After all, Jesus told us, "If you then, who are evil, know how to give good gifts to your children, how much more will the heavenly Father give the Holy Spirit to those who ask him!" (Luke 11:13). There are many such stories, far too many to discount, and more than enough to encourage us to continued prayer, should we grow weary of it.

We must, of course, remain open to the various ways in which God's work is manifested, and increased love is always the most important evidence of divine activity. When people pray for healing, most are praying for a cure. They should not be discouraged in this quest, and especially when healing is understood holistically, with the medical arts as a full partner. As Orthodox theologian Paul Meyendorff observed, the use of oil within the classic healing rite (see James 5:13-16) may be seen as a ritual affirmation of the healing arts. Given this interpretation of anointing, the rite itself witnesses against attempts to place prayer and the medicinal arts in an adversarial relationship with each other.[8] It may help us, however, to allow for a distinction between healing and cure.[9]

Another of my Order of Saint Luke colleagues, Brother Timothy J. Crouch, died in March of 2005 after battling esophageal cancer for about a year and a half. At his request, I spent a weekend with him in November 2004 in order to plan his funeral. He was preparing to die, yet many continued to pray for him, as did I. For what were we praying? He helped us to sort it out. Perhaps ironically, he had been involved in the development of the order's original healing rite,[10] and that service influenced the shape of the "A Service of Healing I" that eventually appeared in *The United Methodist Book of Worship*.[11] In an interview published a month and a half before his death, he discussed his experience of receiving the ministry of others who were praying for him, sometimes using prayers that he had composed: "At times when I have been at my lowest, the most devoid of resource, I actually experience touch—hands and arms holding me. I can only interpret that as people praying for me."[12] While he drew a distinction between healing and cure, he insisted that God was at work and, moreover, that the prayers were a blessing not only to him but also to those who offered them.

Again, there are many such stories, not always ending with a cure but many times with healing. As James insisted, the prayer of the faithful is effective (James 5:16). God also works in yet wider contexts, which leads to my next assertion.

Assertion #3: Through Our Praying, God Works to Change Institutions, Communities, and Nations

Through our praying, God works to change institutions, communities, and nations, although the progress may occur in small, incremental steps.

The Reverend Dr. Marci Pounders, an Episcopal priest, works as a palliative care chaplain. When she was eighteen years old, she discerned a vocation to pray for the healing of others, a call that eventually led to her chaplaincy. As a priest, she understands and believes in a vocation to intercessory prayer that belongs to the whole church, but hers is a particularly strong and focused one. We discussed these more intense vocations earlier in the book (chapter 3), and hers appears to be such a calling. At the least, she spends more time on it than many others do, including some fellow priests. For a time, she led a Wednesday evening healing service at her parish, a service that her rector could complete in about twenty minutes. The same service characteristically took Marci forty-five minutes, with much of the difference spent in praying for people. When she apologized to her parishioners, they told her, "Oh, no, we like it this way."[13]

"I'm very committed to healing ministry," she told me, while also insisting that death is part of God's process. As she understands it, her work as a chaplain is to help persons die in peace, as fully reconciled to God and loved ones as possible.[14] She has been a conversation partner over a number of years, and thus I sought her insights for this book. In midsummer 2010, I shared with her that I was moving toward heart surgery, and she said to me, "I'll bet you didn't expect to become the subject of your own research." Indeed that was so, but I was glad when she became one of many who prayed for me throughout that particular journey.

Palliative care and hospice care values can stand at odds with a medical profession inclined to fight death as hard as possible, at odds with a culture that tries its best to avoid thinking about death. There is something of a conundrum here. Most of the time, we want our physicians and health-care professionals to fight death on our behalf, and to do so aggressively, using all of their skills and insights. Why else submit to heart surgery or, for that matter, take antibiotics? Most of the time they are wonderfully good at what they do, and thanks be to God. Ultimately, however, physicians and medicine cannot beat death. So then, when to quit the fight, and how? These are the questions that she, her palliative care colleagues, and many others ask. In an article that appeared in the *Journal of Palliative Medicine*, she describes a difficult and impersonal reality endured by many, often toward the end of life, with machines and tubes, too much noise, and difficult smells. Drawing on a reference from *Star Trek*, she wrote about her experience of sitting at a dying patient's bed in the ICU, "I feel as if I am on the deck of an enormous spaceship, holding the hand of a carbon unit reduced to a robotic piece of the 'Borg Collective.' If 'resistance is futile,' . . . we didn't get the memo."[15]

In that same article, she describes a church mission trip during which she was able to attend a Honduran woman in the final moments of her life. The woman was surrounded by loved ones, yet without the machines. After prayer, she quietly and peacefully slipped away.[16] Such a dignified, even simple death is the vision toward which Chaplain Marci and other colleagues work and pray. Little by little, such prayerful witness care can change institutions, making them a bit more modest in the face of death. At the least, it presents them with another possibility.[17]

The various ways in which we pray for our campus affects it, changing our relationship to it. Indeed, I work in the midst of two related institutional realms, each of which faces a significantly changing reality: the church and the university. We never know what the future holds for us. Some of these institutions will change, others may realign themselves, and still others may remain much the same as they are now, at least for a while. I may need to learn how to teach online classes, or push myself to the point where I am able to teach in Spanish as well as in English. Who knows but God? The problem is not change, but rather anxious responses in the face of it. Praying in and for both institutions, loving them as they are and as they can be, seems to be the best way forward, a dynamic that will change both those who pray and the institutions, even if little by little.

In like manner, prayers in the streets of Dayton have made that a different community with different life-giving relationships. A similar dynamic, rooted in the vision of gentler nonviolent relationships, can be known within nations and among them. In ways like these, God's people imagine a new heaven and a new earth, all the while praying toward it. And it begins to take shape.

A More Open-Ended Assertion: We Will Never Know About All That God Has Done

I have now made three relatively modest assertions about the effects of our praying. All may be argued and none can be proved. We will, of course, never know the full extent of God's work through our praying, not to mention the full extent of what God does through the rest of our witness. What good comes from celebrating the Eucharist, from reading and studying the scriptures, and from preaching? We do not know all that these practices do or exactly how. Most pastors and teachers have some sense of this spiritual dynamic, and are reminded of it when a former student or parishioner, perhaps long forgotten, relates how something we shared with them helped them, perhaps even effecting a turning point. I sense that our prayers work in a similar manner. My friend Roberto L. Gómez, a retired pastor, related a story from a revival service that he was asked to preach many years ago. He felt led to pray "that someone here be able to stop drinking." Several years later, a man told him that he was present that day, heard the prayer, began recovery from his alcoholism, and then several months later stopped selling alcohol in his convenience store. In like manner, he told me about his conversations with a terminally ill woman in the weeks before her death and subsequent funeral. She asked him to offer prayer at the funeral, specifically that someone be converted to Christ. Although the service took place at a funeral home—not exactly the ideal place for an altar call—he prayed as she asked, after which he issued an invitation to faith. He said, "I don't know what I would've done had someone come forward there." But later, someone told him that she had, in fact, come to faith in response to that invitation.[18] Admittedly, such testimony is difficult to verify, as is most of our testimony about the effects of the church's prayer. On such matters faith speaks to faith, and those inclined to believe will believe. But given active faith in the grace of God, such witness is absolutely plausible. Again, we will never know all of the good that God does in and through our prayers.

I think of my father. As I said earlier (chapter 3), his praying became much bolder as he moved deeper into his retirement. On one occasion, he and my mother, Joanne, went to State College, Pennsylvania, to watch a first-round NCAA women's basketball tournament game featuring the University of Connecticut Huskies, my mother's favorite team. Connecticut won, as they usually do. The morning after the game, they were eating breakfast at a local restaurant when a woman wearing a UConn sweatshirt passed by their table. He asked her, "How did you like the game last night?" Reflecting on that encounter, he wrote,

> I assumed that this stranger was in town for the game, but was badly mistaken.
>
> A few minutes later she returned to our table and shared her story. Her daughter was a Penn State student. The day before she and her daughter had attended the funeral of the daughter's fiancé in Pittsburgh. He had lost a ten-year battle with leukemia. I said to her, "Would you like me to pray with you?" She said, "Yes." I stood up, and put my arm around her shoulder. She placed her head against my shoulder, and we prayed. When the prayer ended, she said "thank you," and we parted.[19]

He never saw her again, and so we can never know what effect, if any, his prayer had on her. If it helped get her through the day, perhaps that was enough. We simply do not know the end of it. We do, of course, know God.

In this book we have been presenting "a baptismal theology for the church's intercessory work." Imagine, then, the prayers that the church offers during the baptismal rite itself, and especially at the laying on of hands. In some churches, that gesture is reserved to the priest or bishop,[20] while in my United Methodist context, the rubric says that "the pastor . . . [and] other persons" may join in the laying on of hands. While a laying on of hands by the full congregation may prove unwieldy, those who remain in the pews could extend their hands toward the baptizand, in blessing, as the following prayer is offered:

The Holy Spirit work within you,
That being born through water and the Spirit
You may be a faithful disciple of Jesus Christ. Amen.[21]

If you do not practice such a corporate laying on of hands in your congregation, consider beginning the practice at the earliest opportunity. Whether or not you do this particular gesture, the congregation may join the prayer through their "Amen."[22]

Think about the implications of that prayer, along with the various other blessings that the congregation invokes on those it baptizes, either in that first sacramental moment or later as persons continue to pray for them and for the whole church. We offer prayers of blessing for them at confirmation and other renewals of the Baptismal Covenant. We pray when children are sent to church camp or when youth and their chaperones depart on a mission trip. We pray for them at graduations, at weddings, at ordinations. Less publicly, parents, grandparents, and other faithful Christians pray for them in secret—for us—usually without our knowing it. Who, besides God, can know what effect those prayers bring to bear in their lives and, indeed, in ours? This corporate laying on of hands was not a part of the church's rite at the time of my baptism; nevertheless, I sense the prayers of the faithful at work in my life, resonating within me in ways that I can only begin to understand. Some of these prayers were offered before I was born, and many by persons who have long since died, but in Christ, the prayers continue. None of it is lost.

In like manner, who, besides God, knows what power and blessing is set in motion when God's faithful exercise their baptismal vocation to intercede for the protection of those who are abused, or in defense of that odd child facing bullies on the grade school playground? Besides God, who knows what good it does when we pray for public school teachers, and coaches of youth sports teams, and, for that matter, for blessing on the work of veterinarians and plumbers? Do they somehow gain an inkling of their dignity as God's servants, of the good that they might do in and through their work? Or, do they somehow find strength to persevere when they think about quitting? We simply do not know the full effect of our prayers, but we have heard God's commandment to pray, and we have begun to perceive our invitation to join God's mission, and so we pray with boldness. We don't know the full effect of our praying, but we do know the immensity of God's power and the depth of God's love, and so we pray. Knowing that God is at work should be more than enough. Through our baptism, we enter God's living waters, and our work of prayer participates in their mysterious, world-shaping flow.

Notes

Introduction: To the Spirit and Toward the World

1. Sister Donna Liette, CPPS, phone interview by author, March 4, 2010.

2. Sister Canice Werner, interview by author, March 24, 2012. Unfortunately, Sister Dorothy, who lived well into her nineties, died only a few weeks before I visited the community to conduct interviews. But Sister Canice kept the story alive. Sister Canice died April 22, 2013. I give thanks to God for her witness, and also for the opportunity to hear it directly from her.

3. Werner interview, March 24, 2012.

4. Ibid.

5. Ibid.

6. Constitution on the Sacred Liturgy (*Sacrosanctum Concilium*), December 4, 1963, accessed August 28, 2013, http://www.vatican.va/archive/hist_councils/ii_vatican_council/documents/vat-ii_const_19631204_sacrosanctum-concilium_en.html.

7. Virgil C. Funk, "The Liturgical Movement (1830–1969)," in *The New Dictionary of Sacramental Worship*, ed. Peter E. Fink (Collegeville, MN: Liturgical Press, 1990), 695–715.

8. Constitution on the Sacred Liturgy, ¶14.

9. Ibid., ¶10.

10. In *The Book of Hymns: Official Hymnal of The United Methodist Church* (Nashville: United Methodist Publishing House, 1966), the post-sanctus begins with reference to the Passion (selection 830, p. 15). While put into service in 1966, the drafting work on that hymnal was essentially completed by the time *SC* was released, and thus it was not affected by it. In its essential form and content, the Communion rite from the 1552 version of *The Book of Common Prayer* remained the ritual form of the church.

The church's next hymnal, published in 1989, was heavily influenced by Vatican II and the liturgical movement. In *The United Methodist Hymnal* (Nashville: United Methodist Publishing House, 1989), the post-sanctus begins with a summary of the entire ministry of Jesus, "Your Spirit anointed him to preach good news to the poor, to proclaim release to the captives," and so on (pp. 9–10). Christ's death and resurrection are by no means overlooked, but they are placed in a wider narrative context, one that is consistent with the structure of the Gospels.

11. "The Baptismal Covenant I," in *The United Methodist Book of Worship* (Nashville: United Methodist Publishing House, 1992), 88.

12. "A Service of Word and Table I," in *United Methodist Hymnal*, 7.

13. *United Methodist Hymnal*, 877, 879.

14. "Service of Word and Table I," also "An Order of Sunday Worship Using the Basic Pattern," in *United Methodist Book of Worship*, 24–25, 34–35.

15. *United Methodist Book of Worship*, 495. See Form IV, *The Book of Common Prayer* (New York: Church Hymnal Corporation, 1979), 388–89.

16. "The Order for the Administration of The Sacrament of Holy Communion or Holy Communion," in *Book of Hymns*, 830.

17. Midday and Night offices are provided, in addition to the Morning and Evening offices provided in *The United Methodist Hymnal*. Biddings are provided for Morning, Midday, and Evening. *United Methodist Book of Worship*, 571, 573, 575–76.

18. *United Methodist Book of Worship* , 255, 263–64, 279, 285, 395–400.

19. In Word and Table I, the presider prays, "Pour out your Holy Spirit on us gathered here, and on these gifts of bread and wine. Make them be for us the body and blood of Christ, that we may be for the world the body of Christ, redeemed by his blood." *United Methodist Hymnal*, 10.

20. "The Baptismal Covenant I," *United Methodist Book of Worship*, 92. Also, *United Methodist Hymnal*, 13.

21. I am indebted to Aidan Kavanagh, who mentioned the connection in his *On Liturgical Theology* (New York: Pueblo, 1984), 134–35.

Chapter One: Teach Us to Pray: Formation in the Midst of Practice

1. The Order of Saint Luke is an ecumenical religious order rooted in Methodism and dedicated to liturgical scholarship, education, and practice. For information on the order and its rule, see http://saint-luke.net/, accessed September 12, 2013.

2. Gordon W. Lathrop, *Holy Things: A Liturgical Theology* (Minneapolis: Fortress, 1993), 33.

3. Ibid., 10.

4. Dwight W. Vogel, "What Is Liturgical Theology?" in *Primary Sources of Liturgical Theology: A Reader*, ed. Dwight W. Vogel (Collegeville, MN: Liturgical Press, 2000), 10. According to Vogel, "The full form of the statement (which can be dated 435–42 C.E.) attributed to Prosper of Aquitane, is *ut legem credendi lex statuat supplicandi* ("the law of prayer grounds the law of belief")".

5. For the Anglican Communion, the origins of this pattern are found in the writings of sixteenth-century theologian Richard Hooker, particularly in book 5 of *The Laws of Ecclesiastical Polity*. Methodist theologian Albert Outler restated this dynamic in *The Book*

of Discipline of The United Methodist Church, 1972 (Nashville: United Methodist Publishing House, 1973), "Our Theological Task, ¶70, pp. 75–79. Essentially Outler expanded Hooker's reason category into reason and experience. To the consternation of many, one will often find Outler's schema referenced as "The Wesleyan Quadrilateral." While drawing upon some Wesleyan (and thereby Anglican) themes, it was Outler's construction, not John Wesley's.

Subsequent clarifications place scripture in the primary place within this dialogue, but the point remains that one cannot do adequate theology simply by quoting scripture. Whether or not we admit it, any process of reflecting on scripture involves conversation with previous understandings and practices (i.e., tradition) and reason/experience. Even the rejection of a previous interpretation or practice is an engagement with it. See "Our Theological Task," in *The Book of Discipline of The United Methodist Church, 2012* (Nashville: United Methodist Publishing House, 2012), ¶105.

6. Aidan Kavanagh, *On Liturgical Theology* (New York: Pueblo, 1984), 8.

7. Robert W. Hovda, *Strong, Loving, and Wise: Presiding in Liturgy* (Washington, DC: Liturgical Conference, 1977), 92.

8. Kavanagh, *On Liturgical Theology*, 74–76.

9. *The HarperCollins Study Bible: New Revised Standard Version*, ed. Harold W. Attridge (San Francisco: HarperSanFrancisco, 2006), 1760.

10. Ibid., 1665–66.

11. For an excellent account of the development of the Lord's Prayer as well as its reception and use within Christian history, see the book by Kenneth W. Stevenson, *The Lord's Prayer: A Text in Tradition* (Minneapolis: Fortress, 2004).

12. In the Greek, *basilea*. It is often translated "kingdom," but "reign" may be a more helpful translation, one less bound by the contingent political realities that can stunt the imagination.

13. I ask the question "Who's missing?" in relation to the ministry of home Communion serving, as in "Who is missing from the church's Communion Table?" It is, however, a discernment question that can be applied to much of the church's life and mission. See Mark W. Stamm, *Extending the Table: A Guide for a Ministry of Home Communion Serving* (Nashville: Discipleship Resources, 2009), 22–25.

14. See alternate reading in the New Revised Standard Version.

15. This word *eschatological* is drawn from the Greek word *eschatos*, meaning "last." In theological terms, to speak of eschatology is to speak of "last things," such as the reign of God, the return (or appearing) of Jesus Christ, heaven, and judgment. The key is to realize the Christian dynamic of time, in which the future—the reign of God or last things—appears in our midst, both to redeem and to judge, and sometimes both at once.

16. Wilhelm Mundle, "*epiousios*," in *The New International Dictionary of New Testament Theology*, vol. 1, ed. Colin Brown (Grand Rapids: Zondervan, 1975), 251.

17. 1 Corinthians 11:24.

18. John 6:32-51.

19. Even under the classic doctrine of transubstantiation, the "accidents" of the bread and wine remain after consecration.

20. Mark W. Stamm, "Intercessions After the Storm," *Sacramental Life* 17, no. 4 (Fall 2005): 47.

21. Ibid., 49.

22. Rowan D. Crews, *Good Lord, Deliver Us: The Praise of God and the Problem of Evil* (Akron, OH: OSL, 2001), 4.

23. Ibid.

24. R. Alan Culpepper. "The Gospel of Luke Introduction, Commentary, and Reflections," in *The New Interpreter's Bible*, vol. 10, *Luke-Acts* Nashville: Abingdon, 1995), 236.

25. Ibid., 237.

26. *The United Methodist Book of Worship*, 88.

Chapter Two: Living Water from the Font

1. Ontology—"from the Greek *on*, 'being,' and *logos*, 'study' "—is the branch of philosophy that concerns itself with the nature of being, or "being as being." Donald K. McKim, *The Westminster Dictionary of Theological Terms* (Louisville, KY: Westminster John Knox Press, 1996), 195.

2. From the perspective of faith in the work of the Holy Spirit, one may also speak of an ontological change occurring when a person is ordained or, for that matter, when a couple are joined in marriage.

3. *The United Methodist Book of Worship* (Nashville: United Methodist Publishing House, 1992), 87.

4. For further discussion of the dynamics of baptism expressed in this paragraph, see the following: James F. White, *Introduction to Christian Worship*, 3rd ed. (Nashville: Abingdon, 2000), chap. 8, 203–28; Laurence Hull Stookey, *Baptism: Christ's Act in the Church* (Nashville: Abingdon, 1982); Mark W. Stamm, *Sacraments and Discipleship: Understanding Baptism and the Lord's Supper in a United Methodist Context* (Ashland City, TN: OSL, 2013; orig. publ. 2001, Nashville: Discipleship Resources).

5. This phrase, of course, is drawn from the Apostles' Creed, historically the profession of faith used at baptism. See *United Methodist Book of Worship*, 89.

6. Augustine of Hippo, "Baptism and Original Sin," in *Enchiridion,* XIII (421), trans. Albert C. Outler, *Library of Christian Classics*, vol. 7 (Philadelphia: Westminster, 1955), 365–68.

7. As Albert Outler asserts, John Wesley's 1756 treatise is an (unacknowledged) abridgement of a baptismal treatise published earlier by his father, Samuel, three years before his birth. While clearly not original to John Wesley, its publication under his name constitutes an endorsement of its views, which also were not particularly original (so to speak) to Samuel. See *John Wesley*, ed. Albert C. Outler (New York: Oxford University Press, 1964), 317.

8. John Wesley, "On Baptism," in Outler, *John Wesley*, 321.

9. Ibid.

10. "This Holy Mystery: A United Methodist Understanding of Holy Communion," in *The Book of Resolutions of The United Methodist Church, 2004* (Nashville: United Methodist Publishing House, 2004). In particular, see the section "Christ Is Calling You," pp. 898–903.

11. "Invitation to Christ," document approved by the 217th General Assembly, Presbyterian Church, USA, June 2006, pp. 18, 22, 28, 30–31, 40, etc.

12. After some discussion at the 2012 General Convention of the Episcopal Church, canon 17.7 remains: "No baptized person shall be eligible to receive Holy Communion in the Church." *Constitution & Canons: Together with the Rules of Order, for the government of the Protestant Episcopal Church in the United States of America, otherwise known as The Episcopal Church,* Adopted and Revised in General Convention, 2012, p. 59.

13. Mark W. Stamm, *Let Every Soul Be Jesus' Guest: A Theology of the Open Table* (Nashville: Abingdon, 2006).

14. Sara Miles, *Take This Bread: A Radical Conversion* (New York: Ballantine, 2007), 58.

15. There are exceptions; see, for instance, Aidan Kavanagh, *On Liturgical Theology* (New York: Pueblo, 1984), 134–35.

16. Peter (and the writer of Acts) assumed that David was the writer of the Psalms, even if much contemporary scholarship does not support that conviction.

17. In the other baptismal stories in Acts, noted earlier, there is almost always some reference to fellowship that emerged following the baptism. After the baptism, Saul/Paul "[took] some food [and] for several days he was with the disciples in Damascus" (Acts 9:19).

After Peter baptized the Gentile Cornelius, whose very house he had been loath to enter, "they invited him to stay for several days" (Acts 10:48), and we might assume that Peter and others did so.

After Lydia and her household were baptized, she said to Paul and his companions, "If you have judged me to be faithful to the Lord, come and stay at my home." And we're told that they did so (Acts 16:15). In like manner, after baptizing the Philippian jailer and his household, Paul and Silas ate with them (Acts 16:34).

After helping the Ephesian Christians to attain a fuller understanding of baptism, Paul stayed in the region for two years (Acts 19:10).

The baptism of the Ethiopian eunuch presents a challenge to this pattern of baptism followed by fellowship, since we have the odd and intriguing story of Philip being snatched up by the Spirit and sent to Azotus immediately following the eunuch's baptism (Acts 8:40). Clearly, there was no postbaptismal breaking of bread between them. However, the fact that the eunuch's story is preserved at least suggests that he eventually found fellowship in a community of believers.

18. See use of this same phrase, "the breaking of the bread," in Luke 24:35. In that text, it is used in reference to the classic fourfold eucharistic pattern—took, blessed, broke, and gave. "When he was at the table with them, [Jesus] took bread, blessed and broke it, and gave it to them" (Luke 24:30). See the same pattern in the Lukan narrative of the institution of the Lord's Supper (Luke 22:19).

19. Dwight W. Vogel, *Food for Pilgrims: A Journey with Saint Luke* (Akron, OH: OSL, 1996), 9.

20. Stamm, *Let Every Soul Be Jesus' Guest*, 3–13.

21. Richard Hooker, "Whether Baptism by Women Be True Baptism, Good and Effectual to Them That Receive It," in *Of the Laws of Ecclesiastical Polity*, book 5 (1597), chap. 62.

22. *The First Apology of Justin Martyr*, in *The Ante-Nicene Fathers, Translations of the Writings of the Fathers down to A.D. 325*, ed. Alexander Roberts and James Donaldson, vol. 1 (Grand Rapids: Eerdmans, n.d.), chap. 61, p. 183.

23. Ibid., chap. 62–64, pp. 183–85.

24. Ibid., chap. 65, p. 185.

25. Ibid., chap. 61, p. 183.

26. Ibid., chap. 65, p. 185.

27. Ibid.

28. Ibid.

29. *Didache*, 9, trans. Cyril C. Richardson, in *Early Christian Fathers, Library of Christian Classics,* vol. 1 (New York: Macmillan, 1970), 175.

30. See the "General Introduction" to *The Treatise on The Apostolic Tradition of St. Hippolytus of Rome, Bishop and Martyr*, ed. Gregory Dix and Henry Chadwick (London: Alban, 1937), xi–xxxv.

31. Paul F. Bradshaw, Maxwell E. Johnson, and L. Edward Phillips. *The Apostolic Tradition: A Commentary* Harold W. Attridge (Minneapolis: Fortress, 2002), xi, 9, 14 (hereafter *AT*).

32. *AT* 16, p. 88.

33. *AT* 17:1-2, p. 96.

34. *AT* 27:1, p. 144.

35. The postbaptismal anointing is thought by some to be a ritual ancestor of confirmation. See, for example, Gregory Dix and Henry Chadwick, *The Treatise on The Apostolic Tradition of St. Hippolytus of Rome, Bishop and Martyr* (London: Alban, 1992), 38–39. They use "Confirmation" as their heading for section 22, which describes the postbaptismal episcopal laying on of hands and anointing with oil.

Aidan Kavanagh takes issue with Dix and Chadwick, insisting that confirmation, as such, is not present in *AT*. He understood the laying on of hands with anointing as a simple dismissal rite, or *missa*, which eventually developed into the confirmation rite. See Kavanagh, *Confirmation: Origins and Reform* (New York: Pueblo, 1988), 51, 67–70.

36. *AT* 21:23-27, pp. 118, 120.

37. For evidence in support of this claim, see the section titled "Passionate (Even Indignant) Responses" on pp. 98–103 of my *Let Every Soul Be Jesus' Guest.*

38. *AT* 35:42, p. 178.

39. J. D. C. Fisher, *Christian Initiation: Baptism in the Medieval West,*

A Study in the Disintegration of the Primitive Rite of Initiation (Chicago: Hillenbrand, 2007 orig. publ. 1965, Alcuin Club, UK), 8.

40. Ibid., 185.

41. Ibid., 186–94.

42. The 1549 BCP was heavily critiqued, particularly by those who favored a more extensive Protestant reformation of the church's rites, and so a revised version was released in 1552, in which major changes were made in the rite for the Lord's Supper / Holy Communion. The death of the Protestant king Edward VI in 1553 and the subsequent succession of the Catholic queen Mary Tudor meant that the 1552 book was in use but for a short time. Following Mary's death and the coronation of Elizabeth I in 1558, a 1559 version of the BCP was issued, which retained many of the revisions of 1552, but with some compromises and a somewhat less strident tone. This book remained until the Commonwealth period in the mid-seventeenth century, during which it was replaced by A Directory for the Public Worship of God (the Westminster Directory) in 1644. After restoration of the monarchy, the 1662 BCP became the official liturgy of the realm, and it remains so to this day. As such, it was the prayer book in use during John Wesley's lifetime (1703–1791). As noted, there were changes in the ritual texts for the Lord's Supper, and especially from 1549 to 1552, but the baptismal texts we will discuss remained essentially the same across the four versions of the BCP.

43. "Of the Administration of Public Baptism to Be Used in the Church," in The Book of Common Prayer, 1549, accessed October 3, 2013, http://justus.anglican.org/resources/bcp/1549/Baptism_1549.htm. In order to help the reader better follow the argument, here and in subsequent references to the 1549 BCP I have updated the spellings to contemporary American usage. The first line looked like this: "DEARE beloved, forasmuche as all men bee conceyved and borne in sinne, and that no manne borne in synne . . ." I do take to heart the observation of my professor John E. Booty, who reminded our class that reading this text in its original spelling helps one remember that it is, in fact, a sixteenth-century document. I will leave it to you, however, to check the website for the sixteenth-century spellings.

44. "Of the Administration of Public Baptism to Be Used in the Church," in The Book of Common Prayer, 1549.

45. "Confirmation, Wherein Is Contained a Catechism for Children," in ibid.

46. "Presenting the Lord's Prayer," in *Rite of Christian Initiation of Adults, Study Edition* (Chicago: Liturgy Training Publications, 1988), ¶¶178–80, pp. 111–12 (hereafter *RCIA*).

47. *RCIA*, ¶241, p. 150. For the full baptismal rite that precedes the intercessions, see ¶¶218 through 240, pp. 127–50.

48. David Yamane and Sarah MacMillen, *Real Stories of Christian Initiation: Lessons for and from the RCIA* (Collegeville, MN: Liturgical Press, 2006), 26, 42, 52, 92, 97.

49. *RCIA*, ¶75.3, pp. 37–38.

50. Brian Kaylor, "Anniversary of Bailey Smith's Harmful Moment in Baptist-Jewish Relations," August 23, 2010, accessed October 6, 2013, http://www.ethicsdaily.com/news.php?viewStory=16564.

51. "Invitation to Christ," , 9.

52. Such renovations must, of course, take architectural and engineering issues into account as well as theological and aesthetic considerations. Regarding new immersion fonts placed within existing buildings, Regina Kuehn wrote, "A structural engineer may be consulted to determine whether the floor is strong enough to carry the weight of the building material in addition to the weight of the water." The floor may need to be reinforced or otherwise strengthened. Kuehn, *A Place for Baptism* (Chicago: Liturgy Training Publications, 1992), 95–96.

53. The funeral pall is a large white cloth, often embroidered with a cross, which is placed over the casket for the funeral service. Normally owned by the church, it may be used for the funeral of any member, and thus is a sign of equality among the sisters and brothers—regardless of the quality of the casket, everyone in the church comes to their funeral vested in the same manner. The pall should be understood as a baptismal garment, signifying the deceased's identity as a child of God and brother or sister in the faith.

54. I am indebted to C. Michael Hawn for the term *cyclic songs* and for any insights I now have about musical forms suitable for movement over against those that might be used when the congregation is standing or sitting within the nave. He suggests that churches develop a repertoire of forty to fifty such songs for use on ritual occasions similar to the one that I have described here. Hawn, *One Bread, One Body: Exploring Cultural Diversity in* Worship (Bethesda, MD: Alban Institute, 2003), 171.

55. *Didache*, 7, in *Early Christian Fathers*, 174.

56. Miles, *Take This Bread*, 79–80.

Chapter Three: What Does This Vocation Look Like?

1. "The Baptismal Covenant I," in *The United Methodist Book of Worship* (Nashville: United Methodist Publishing House, 1992), 88.

2. "A Service of Christian Marriage I," in ibid., 120.

3. Typically, pilgrims such as our group from Perkins are invited to join the Taizé Community for a full week.

4. The word *office* comes from the Latin *officium,* for "duty" or "service."

5. For a recording of the bells of Taizé, check the following URL, accessed October 29, 2013: http://www.taize.fr/en_article681.html.

6. Jason Brian Santos, *A Community Called Taizé: A Story of Prayer, Worship, and Reconciliation* (Downers Grove, IL: InterVarsity Press, 2008).

7. Timothy Fry, ed., *RB 1980, The Rule of St. Benedict in Latin and English with Notes* (Collegeville, MN: Liturgical Press, 1981), chap. 48.1, p. 249. The rule says, "Idleness is the enemy of the soul. Therefore, the brothers should have specific periods for manual labor as well as for prayerful reading."

8. *Rule of St. Benedict in Latin and English with Notes,* chap. 16.1, p. 211. "The Prophet says: *Seven times a day have I praised you* (Ps. 118 [119]:164). We will fulfill this sacred number of seven if we satisfy our obligation of service at Lauds, Prime, Terce, Sext,

None, Vespers, and Compline." According to Timothy Fry's account, the Rule of St. Benedict emerged in sixth-century Italy (p. 65).

9. The Order of Saint Luke is a dispersed (i.e., nonresidential) ecumenical religious order of women and men, married and single persons, ordained and lay. Rooted in Methodism, the order is dedicated to sacramental and liturgical scholarship, education, and practice. For information on the order and its Rule of Life and Service, see the website (accessed October 29, 2013), http://saint-luke.net/.

10. Dwight W. Vogel, ed. and compiler, *The Book of Offices and Services of the Order of Saint Luke,* 4th ed. (Ashland, TN: OSL, 2012), 34.

11. Ibid., 36.

12. Ibid., 38.

13. For full examples of these offices, with explanations for each, see ibid., 27–64.

14. See "The Preface," in The Book of Common Prayer (1549), accessed October 30, 2013, http://justus.anglican.org/resources/bcp/1549/front_matter_1549.htm#Preface.

15. *The Book of Common Prayer* (New York: Church Hymnal Corporation, 1979), 37–135.

16. Paul F. Bradshaw, *Two Ways of Praying* (Nashville: Abingdon, 1995), 13–26.

17. "Diocese of Fort Worth to ordain second woman as priest," *News Around the Episcopal Diocese of Fort Worth*, accessed December 5, 2009, http://www.episcopaldiocese fortworth.org/newsindiocese/120109-gitaneordination.htm.

18. ClayOla Gitane, interview by author, March 2, 2010.

19. For a short description of the practice, see *United Methodist Book of Worship*, 445. For a longer description of the practice, see the following: Su Yon Pak, Unzu Lee, Jung Ha Kim, and Myung Ji Cho, "Fervent Prayer: The Practice of Praying Together," chap. 4 in *Singing the Lord's Song in a New Land: Korean American Practices of Faith* (Louisville, KY: Westminster John Knox Press, 2005), 35–44.

20. Ibid., 36.

21. Observation, October 4, 2005.

22. Observation, December 30, 2011.

23. Pak, Lee, Kim, and Cho, "Fervent Prayer," 39.

24. "Baptismal Covenant I," , 88.

25. Conversation with author, April 20, 2010.

26. Conversation with author, September 29, 2009.

27. Conversation with author, October 28, 2009.

28. For an expansion of this perspective, see the following article by Philip Jenkins: "Taking Back the Night," *Christian Century* 126, no. 2 (January 27, 2009): 45.

29. See "The Transitus: An Order for the Time of Passage through Death to Life," *The Book of Offices and Services, The Order of Saint Luke* (4th ed.), 81–84. The order may be used prior to death, immediately after death, or on memorial occasions.

30. Interview by author, October 28, 2009.

31. Interview by author, June 16, 2010.

32. E-mail to author, April 22, 2010.

33. Interview by author, April 20, 2010.

34. Interview by author, October 28, 2009.

35. Two conversations with author, July 20, 2010.

36. John W. Stamm, "Reflections of a Veteran Retiree," unpublished manuscript for a talk delivered to the banquet for retirees and ordinands at the Central Pennsylvania Conference, meeting at Messiah College, Grantham, Pennsylvania, June 9, 2006.

37. John Wesley, letter to James Hervey, March 20, 1739, in *John Wesley*, ed. Albert C. Outler (New York: Oxford University Press, 1964), 72.

38. For the story of the Baseball Berakah, and the text of the prayer, see my article "Pray Ball? On the Serious Liturgical Challenge of Giving Thanks for Baseball," *Doxology* 28 (2011): 72–93.

39. Accounts of this story about this prayer service, written by me, have appeared in various forms in the following two venues: "Holy Hanging Around: On Formation for Baptismal Living among United Methodists," *Pray Tell: Worship, Wit, and Wisdom*, blog sponsored by Liturgical Press, posted November 29, 2010, http://www.praytellblog.com/index.php/2010/11/29/holy-hanging-around-on-formation-for-baptismal-living/; and "Holy Hanging Around, on Formation for Baptismal Living among United Methodists," reprint of blog post to *Pray Tell* with "Afterword," *Sacramental Life* 23, no. 3 (Summer 2011): 5–18.

Chapter Four: Intercession and Forming Disciples

1. As noted in the previous chapter, my reflections on the prayer service that my students held for me have appeared as follows: "Holy Hanging Around: On Formation for Baptismal Living among United Methodists," *Pray Tell: Worship, Wit, and Wisdom*, blog sponsored by Liturgical Press, posted November 29, 2010,

http://www.praytellblog.com/index.php/2010/11/29/holy-hanging-around-on-formation-for-baptismal-living/; and "Holy Hanging Around: On Formation for Baptismal Living among United Methodists," reprint of blog post to *Pray Tell* with "Afterword," *Sacramental Life* 23, no. 3 (Summer 2011): 5–18.

2. Foremost among these efforts has been the work of David Lowes Watson and Steven W. Manskar. Watson provides an extensive historical account of the class meeting process in *The Early Methodist Class Meeting* (Nashville: Discipleship Resources, 1992). Manskar provides an outline and guide for a contemporary *praxis* of the class meeting in his *Accountable Discipleship: Living in God's Household* (Nashville: Discipleship Resources, 2000).

3. John Wesley, "The Nature, Design, and General Rules of the United Societies in London, Bristol, Kingswood, and Newcastle upon Tyne (1743)," in *The Words of John Wesley*, vol. 9, *The Methodist Societies: History, Nature, and Design* (Nashville: Abingdon, 1989), 67–73.

4. Paul F. Bradshaw, Maxwell E. Johnson, and L. Edward Phillips, "Concerning Crafts and Professions," in *The Apostolic Tradition: A Commentary*, ed. Harold W. Attridge (Minneapolis: Fortress, 2002), 88, 90.

5. Ibid., 96.

6. John Wilkinson, ed. and trans., *Egeria's Travels to the Holy Land*, rev. ed. (Jerusalem: Ariel, 1981), 45.1–4, 143–44.

7. *Rite of Christian Initiation of Adults* (Chicago: Liturgy Training Publications, 1988), ¶75.2, p. 37.

8. Ibid., ¶75.2, p. 37.

9. Ibid., ¶76, p. 38.

10. Ibid., ¶241, p. 150.

11. Owen F. Cummings, *Deacons and the Church* (New York: Paulist Press, 2004), 22–29.

12. See translation in Lucien Deiss, *Springtime of the Liturgy: Liturgical Texts of the First Four Centuries* (Collegeville, MN: Liturgical Press, 1979), 175.

13. Wilkinson, *Egeria's Travels to the Holy Land*, 24:5, 124.

14. For a general discussion of the office of the deacon within the Roman tradition, see Cummings, *Deacons and the Church*.

15. Ibid., 50.

16. James F. White, ed., *John Wesley's Prayer Book: The Sunday Service of the Methodists in North America (1784)* (Cleveland, OH: OSL, 1991), 284–85. Wesley, in turn, was drawing upon the 1662 version of The Book of Common Prayer.

17. Cummings, *Deacons and the Church*, 51–52.

18. According to *The Book of Discipline of The United Methodist Church, 1992* (Nashville: United Methodist Publishing House, 1992), reflecting the rules in force immediately prior to the 1996 General Conference, requirements for admission to full Annual Conference membership and ordination as elder included "(previous election) as probationary members and ordained deacons" (¶424.2, p. 224).

The Book of Discipline of The United Methodist Church, 1996 (Nashville: United Methodist Publishing House, 1996) describes two complementary ordained orders, deacon and elder, with no transitional or complementary ordination for elder (¶¶303 and 326, pp. 170–71, 196–99). These rules supporting the two complementary orders have been maintained in subsequent editions of the *Discipline*. See *The Book of Discipline of The United Methodist Church, 2012* (Nashville: United Methodist Publishing House, 2012), ¶¶305 and 335, pp. 220–21, 259–62.

19. Current legislation in *The Book of Discipline of The United Methodist Church* allows a limited exception under which a deacon may preside at the Eucharist, but only if no elder is present. The exception must be specifically requested and for particular circumstances (*The Book of Discipline—2012*, ¶328, p. 246).

20. Under United Methodist polity, elders are subject to the appointment of their bishop, and thus are said to be itinerant ministers. Such itinerant ministry has been a hallmark of Methodist polity from its inception, and the refusal to participate has been seen as a serious breach of covenant. Under the changes in our understanding of ordination as instituted in 1996, however, deacons are no longer required to itinerate. See *The Book of Discipline—2012*, ¶338, pp. 264–65. As much as the distinctions between the

work of its elders and deacons restored the possibility of complementary ordained orders within the wider baptismal covenant, this provision that excuses deacons from itinerant ministry constitutes a regressive step in our understanding of ministry and baptismal vocation. In the current system, becoming an ordained deacon could be a way to serve as an ordained minister without having to itinerate in consultation with one's bishop. In a biblical understanding of calling, however, who answers a call from God and remains where he or she was before hearing it? It did not happen with Abraham and Sarah, with Moses, with Mary, or with the apostles, and likely not with us. Those who hear a call from God must move emotionally and/or intellectually, and sometimes physically; often one must move in all of these ways.

Furthermore, what shall we make of the ancient rubric from *The Apostolic Tradition*, "And let each one of the deacons and subdeacons assist the bishop and let them inform him about everyone who is sick"? Bradshaw, Johnson, and Phillips, "That It Is Proper for the Deacons to Assist the Bishop," in *Apostolic Tradition*, 176.

21. The theory in play here is known as systems theory, or Bowen theory, and is often used in counseling relationships, although many see wider applications. See any of the following texts: Edward H. Friedman, *Generation to Generation: Family Process in Church and Synagogue* (New York: Guilford, 1985); Ronald W. Richardson, *Creating a Healthier Church: Family Systems Theory and Congregational Life* ((Minneapolis: Fortress, 1996); Kenneth A. Halstead, *From Stuck to Unstuck: Overcoming Congregational Impasse* (Bethesda, MD: Alban Institute), 1998.

22. The technical name for the "Butterfly Effect" is "sensitive dependence on initial conditions." See James Gleick, *Chaos: Making a New Science* (New York: Penguin, 1987), 20–23.

23. August 3, 2011, conversation with the author.

24. Sara Miles, *Jesus Freak: Feeding, Healing, Raising the* Dead (San Francisco: Jossey-Bass, 2010), 166.

25. Sara Miles, conversation with the author, August 4, 2011.

26. Paul Fromberg, conversation with the author, August 4, 2011.

This statement is consistent with Sara Miles' statement that, in many churches, "the font serves as a gate to keep the wrong people away from the feast." Miles, *Take This Bread: A Radical Conversion* (New York: Ballantine, 2007), 79.

27. See discussion in chapter 2, pages 41–46.

28. Paul Fromberg, conversation with the author, August 4, 2011.

29. Sara Miles, conversation with the author, August 4, 2011.

30. Here, Miles's language echoes that which she used in her book *Jesus Freak*, 125–61.

31. For still photos of from liturgies at St. Gregory's, see "Photos of Our Liturgies," on their website (accessed November 18, 2013), http://www.saintgregorys.org/worship/liturgy_section/995/.For video and commentary on the dance movements within their liturgy, see *Dancing With God: Worship at Saint Gregory's* (San Francisco: Flying Carp Productions, 2000).

32. *Morning Prayer, St. Gregory of Nyssa Episcopal Church*, 2011, 6.

33. Sara Miles, e-mail to author, September 14, 2014.

34. Miles, *Take This Bread*, 253–54.

35. For an excellent account of Ambrose' teaching, see the book by Craig Alan Satterlee, *Ambrose of Milan's Mystagogical Teaching* (Collegeville, MN: Liturgical Press, 2002).

36. *St. Ambrose "On the Sacraments" and "On the Mysteries" and the Treatise "on the Sacraments,"* trans. T. Thompson, ed. J. H. Stawley (London: SPCK, 1950), 70.

37. Ibid., 72–73.

38. Ibid., 72.

39. For an extensive discussion of the *pedalavium* (footwashing) and its relation to Christian initiation, see Maxwell E. Johnson, *The Rites of Christian Initiation: Their Evolution and Interpretation* (Collegeville, MN: Liturgical Press, 1999), 20–22, 31, 137–40, 157, 196, 198.

40. See Merlin C. Shull and J. E. Miller, *Minister's Manual: Church of the Brethren* (Elgin, IL: Brethren Publishing House, 1940). Saint Ambrose might agree with the reference to sacrament found in "The Service of Feet Washing" (p. 117): "We have come to the time when we shall observe the first of the sacraments instituted by our Lord on the night he spent with his disciples before his crucifixion. Brother . . . will read John 13:1-17."

41. Note the description of the biannual four-week Amish Communion season found in Donald B. Kraybill, Steven M. Nolt, and David L. Weaver-Zercher, *Amish Grace: How Forgiveness Transcended Tragedy* (San Francisco: Jossey-Bass, 2007), 116–22. On the final Sunday of the season, an eight-hour service culminates in Holy Communion followed by footwashing. The preparatory season works in dialogue with each community's local version of the ordnung, the discipline that each member of the church vows to follow when he or she is baptized. Thus, the whole season, including its culminating rites, is a reaffirmation of that baptismal covenant.

42. Laurence Hull Stookey, *Calendar: Christ's Time for the Church* (Nashville: Abingdon, 1996).

43. "A Service of Worship for Holy Thursday Evening," in *The United Methodist Book of Worship* (Nashville: United Methodist Publishing House, 1992), 351, 353.

44. *Book of Common Worship* (Louisville, KY: Westminster/John Knox Press, 1993), 268, 273; *Evangelical Lutheran Worship* (Minneapolis: Augsburg Fortress, 2006), 260.

45. *The Book of Common Prayer* (New York: Church Hymnal Corporation, 1979), 274.

46. Gordon W. Lathrop, *Holy Things: A Liturgical Theology* (Minneapolis: Fortress, 1998), 10, etc.

Chapter Five: Intercession and the Baptismal Covenant

1. I am grateful to my colleague Taylor Burton-Edwards for pointing out this variant translation of the Greek word *hopla*. See variant noted in the New Revised Standard translation.

2. Gordon W. Lathrop, *Holy Things: A Liturgical Theology* (Minneapolis: Fortress, 1993, 1998), 27–31.

3. Kenneth Stevenson, *Jerusalem Revisited: The Liturgical Meaning of Holy Week* (Washington, DC: Pastoral Press, 1988), 5.

4. John Wilkinson, ed. and trans., *Egeria's Travels to the Holy Land* (Jerusalem: Ariel, 1981), 37:4–6, p. 137.

5. Elaine Heath, *We Were the Least of These: Reading the Bible with Survivors of Sexual Abuse* (Grand Rapids: Brazos, 2011), 122–23.

6. *Documents on the Liturgy, 1963–1979, Conciliar, Papal, and Curial Texts* (Collegeville, MN: Liturgical Press, 1982), 600.

7. Ibid. The post–Vatican II church both altered and softened this language. For instance, now prayers are offered "for all in public office, for the unity of Christians, for the Jewish people, for those who do not believe in Christ, and for those who do not believe in God." *The Sacramentary, Approved for use in the Dioceses of the United States of America by the National Conference of Catholic Bishops and Confirmed by the Apostolic See,* English translation prepared by the International Committee on English in the Liturgy (Collegeville, MN: Liturgical Press, 1974), 211–22.

8. *Documents on the Liturgy, 1963–1979,* 600.

9. R. H. Connolly, "Liturgical Prayers of Intercession: The Good Friday *Orationes Solemnes,*" *Journal of Theological Studies* 21 (1920): 231.

10. Anton Baumstark, *Comparative Liturgy,* revised by Bernard Botte, English edition by F. L. Cross (London: Mowbray, 1958), 27. See explanation pp. 27–30.

11. I am indebted to my doctoral mentor, Professor Horace T. Allen Jr., for giving me this insight into the dynamics of John's Passion narrative.

12. *The Book of Common Prayer* (New York: Church Hymnal Corporation, 1979), 277.

13. Ibid., 278–80.

14. *Book of Common Worship* (Louisville, KY: Westminster/John Knox Press, 1993), 283–87.

15. *The Roman Missal, Renewed by Decree of the Most Holy Second Ecumenical Council of the Vatican, Promulgated by Authority of Pope Paul VI and Revised at the Direction of Pope John Paul II* (Collegeville, MN: Liturgical Press, 2011), 316–29.

16. *Evangelical Lutheran Worship* (Minneapolis: Augsburg Fortress, 2006), 263.

17. *The United Methodist Book of Worship* (Nashville: United Methodist Publishing House, 1992), 364.

18. Alyce M. McKenzie, *Novel Preaching: Tips from Top Writers on Crafting Creative Sermons* (Louisville, KY: Westminster John Knox Press, 2010), 137.

19. See these, for example:

The icon from the St. Gregory Antiochian Orthodox Church in Washington, D.C., accessed May 30, 2014, http://www.stgregoryoc.org/article/article-archive/saints-of-the-passion/.

The icon written by Father Theodore Jurewicz at Christ the Savior Orthodox Church in Harrisburg, Pennsylvania, accessed May 30, 2014, http://www.christthesaviourhbg.org/icons.html.

Constantine Cavarnos, *Guide to Byzantine Iconography* (Boston: Holy Transfiguration Monastery, 1993), 170–72.

20. William A. Dyrness, *Senses of the Soul: Art and the Visual in Christian Worship* (Eugene, OR: Cascade Books, 2008), 160. Dyrness notes that while Protestants may use icons in their worship and devotions, they tend to interpret them according to the piety in which they were formed.

21. Elizabeth C. Clephane, "Beneath the Cross of Jesus," 1872, in *The United Methodist Hymnal* (Nashville: United Methodist Publishing House, 1989), 297.

22. African American Spiritual, "Were You There," in *United Methodist Hymnal*, 288.

23. James Montgomery, "Go to Dark Gethsemane," in *United Methodist Hymnal*, 290.

24. See my *Let Every Soul Be Jesus' Guest: A Theology of the Open Table* (Nashville: Abingdon, 2006), 125–39.

25. See also my "Intercessions in an Anti-Docetic Mode as Prepared for the 2011 Order of Saint Luke Retreat," *Sacramental Life* 24, no. 4 (Ordinary Time 2012): 52–59.

26. Stamm, *Let Every Soul Be Jesus' Guest*, 125–27.

27. "Ignatius to the Smyrnaeans," trans. Lightfoot and Harmer, *Apostolic Fathers* (1891 translation), 2:1-3:1, 6:2, accessed July 1, 2011, http://www.earlychristianwritings.com/text/ignatius-smyrnaeans-lightfoot.html.

28. Thomas G. Long, *Accompany Them Singing: The Christian Funeral* (Louisville, KY: Westminster John Knox Press, 2009), 5, 31–32.

29. Marjorie Procter-Smith, *Praying with Our Eyes Open* (Nashville: Abingdon, 1995), 72–73.

30. Stamm, "Intercessions in an Anti-Docetic Mode."

31. *United Methodist Hymnal*, 34.

32. Chris Rose, *1 Dead in Attic* (New York: Simon and Schuster, 2007), 56.

33. To gain a sense of the chaos during Katrina but also after, see Chris Rose's book.

34. Unless otherwise noted, this information from Deacon Clements comes from my on-site conversation and tour with her of March 19, 2010, followed by e-mail exchanges on March 25, 2010, and September 23, 2014.

35. For a photo and video about the wall, see this URL on the St. Anna's website (accessed December 20, 2013): http://www.stannanola.org/photos-videos/victims-of-violence/.

36. From the introduction to "The Prayers of the People," in *The Book of Common Prayer* (1979), 383.

37. See *United Methodist Book of Worship*, 571, 573, 576.

38. Prayers of the people composed by Elaine Clements for September 13, 2009.

39. E-mail, Elaine Clements to the author, July 3, 2010.

40. Ibid.

41. Group interview of vigil participants, March 24, 2012.

42. Ibid.

43. Stamm, *Let Every Soul Be Jesus' Guest,* 139.

44. Undated prayer, Salem Heights Sisters of the Precious Blood, author's file.

45. "Song of Liberation" (For the Twenty-Fifth Anniversary of the Kansas City Province of the Society of the Precious Blood.) Joseph Nassal, CPPS.

46. Sister Donna Liette, phone interview, March 4, 2010.

47. Group interview, March 24, 2012.

48. Ibid.

49. Sister Jeanette Buehler interview, March 23, 2012.

50. Interview with Street Souljahz leader, March 24, 2012.

51. Ibid.

52. Sister Donna Liette, interview, March 4, 2010.

53. Ibid.

54. Sister Jeanette Buehler, interview, March 23, 2012.

55. Survivors interview, March 24, 2012.

56. Mark Danner, *The Massacre at El Mozote* (New York: Random House, 1993), 3–10, 62–84, etc.

57. E-mail to author, December 15, 2007.

58. Much of this material appeared previously in my article ""Intercessions in an Anti-Docetic Mode," 52–59.

59. *Book of Common Prayer* (1979), 395.

60. Ibid., 385–87.

61. Ibid., 383. Compare list of biddings for "Prayers of the People" in the United Methodist orders for Daily Prayer and Praise. *United Methodist Book of Worship* , 571, 573, and 576.

62. "*Kyrie Eleison,*" Taizé, *United Methodist Hymnal* , 484.

Chapter Six: Intercession and the Baptismal Covenant

1. *The United Methodist Book of Worship* (Nashville: United Methodist Publishing House, 1992), 88.

2. Given a postexilic date for the final version of Exodus, it is possible to view the tabernacle narrative as both historical memory and also as vision of God's eschatological intention, that is, of God's intention for Israel beyond the days of the stationary Temple. Waldener Janzen, "Tabernacle," *The New Interpreter's Dictionary of the Bible, S-Z,* vol. 5 (Nashville: Abingdon, 2009), 451–52.

3. "The Supper of the Lord and The Holy Communion, Commonly Called the Mass," in The Book of Common Prayer (1549), accessed June 4, 2014, http://justus.anglican.org/resources/bcp/1549/Communion_1549.htm; "The Holy Eucharist: Rite One," in *The Book of Common Prayer* (New York: Church Hymnal Corporation, 1979), 331; "The Service of Word and Table IV," in *The United Methodist Book of Worship* (Nashville:

United Methodist Publishing House, 1992), 44–45; "The Order for the Administration of the Sacrament of the Lord's Supper or Holy Communion," in *The Book of Hymns: Official Hymnal of The United Methodist Church* (Nashville: United Methodist Publishing House, 1966), 830, p. 12.

4. "The Supper of the Lord and The Holy Communion, Commonly Called the Mass, in The Book of Common Prayer (1549).; "The Holy Eucharist: Rite One," in *The Book of Common Prayer* (1979), 337; "The Service of Word and Table IV," in *The United Methodist Book of Worship* (1992), 49–50; "The Order for the Administration of the Sacrament of the Lord's Supper or Holy Communion," in *The Book of* Hymns, 830, p. 15

5. Both churches, however, retain versions of their previous Communion rituals, and both of these rites include "The Prayer of Humble Access." For United Methodists, see "Service of Word and Table IV," in *United Methodist Book of Worship*, 49–50. For Episcopalians, see *The Book of Common Prayer* (1979), 337.

6. *The United Methodist Book of Worship*, 50; *The Book of Common Prayer* (1979), 337.

7. Even the Episcopal Church's classical Rite I and the United Methodist "Service of Word and Table IV" represent steps forward. The sixteenth-century versions of The Book of Common Prayer also contained stern exhortations warning persons against "unworthy" reception of Holy Communion. Accessed August 4, 2014, http://justus.anglican.org/resources/bcp/1549/Communion_1549.htm.

To review the Catholic rite in use at the time of the Protestant Reformation, see "The Mass," in Bard Thompson, *Liturgies of the Western Church* (Philadelphia: Fortress, 1961), 27–91. To view the various references to sin, unworthiness, and petitions for deliverance from the same, see pp. 57, 59, 65, 77, 79, 81, and 83. It is the dominant theme of the rite.

8. Gordon W. Lathrop, *Holy Things: A Liturgical Theology* (Minneapolis: Fortress, 1993, 1998), 27–31. See earlier discussion in chapter 5.

9. I am grateful to Perkins alumnus Richard Cato for challenging me to clarify this matter during a 2014 Ministers Week presentation.

10. Thomas L. Friedman, *Hot, Flat, and Crowded: Why We Need a Green Revolution, and How It Can Renew America* (New York: Farrar, Straus, 2008).

11. Ibid., 96, 240, etc.

12. Ibid., 119.

13. Ibid., chap. 5, "Global Weirding, Climate Change," 111–39. Barbara Kingsolver uses the same term in her fascinating and provocative novel *Flight Behavior* (New York: Harper, 2012).

14. In addition to the provost's annual choice of a book, SMU had developed the Common Reading Project, in which the incoming freshman class is assigned a book and asked to read it before they arrive on campus. On the afternoon before the Opening Convocation, they meet in assigned groups to discuss the text, led by faculty volunteers drawn from across the university. The annual book choices, chosen by a university committee, address a variety of topics, none of them self-consciously theological. But discerning readers can usually find the theological/intercessory implications in such texts. The Common

Reading Project is a wonderful tradition, one that communities and churches would do well to consider.

15. *Hot, Flat, and Crowded*, 127.

16. Ibid., 127–28.

17. Ibid., 128.

18. Ibid., 128.

19. Ibid., 129.

20. Ibid., 316.

21. Ibid., 315.

22. One can, of course, become overly sentimental in such discussions. We contracted to have our live oak tree trimmed in mid-November of 2013. It needed it, and it seemed like a fortuitous move when a major ice storm in early December caused heavy damage to many trees in our neighborhood. Our tree sustained but minimal damage, in large part because its branches had recently been thinned. But the trimming seemed to disrupt the jays as well as the running track for the squirrels, and in that I felt a sense of loss. In an urban setting, one cannot avoid the tough choices that come with stewardship of a property. Nevertheless, I will stand by my conclusion that it is good to notice what is going on there.

23. Within the Revised Common Lectionary, 1 Corinthians 15:19-26 is the epistle appointed for Easter Sunday, Year C. The earlier part of Paul's discussion of the Resurrection, 1 Corinthians 15:1-11, is appointed for Easter Sunday, Year B.

24. I tell my students that their liturgical education is incomplete until they have participated in an Easter Vigil, and I commend it to my readers as well. For a full text of the order for the Easter Vigil, see *United Methodist Book of Worship*, 368–76. See also *The Book of Common Prayer* (1979), 285–95.

25. The Revised Common Lectionary appoints the following Old Testament texts for the Easter Vigil. I list them here, along with their titles as rendered in *The United Methodist Book of Worship*, 373–75: Genesis 1:1–2:4a (The Creation); Genesis 7:1-5, 11-18; 8:6-18; 9:8-13 (The Covenant Between God and Earth); Genesis 22:1-18 (Abraham's Trust in God); Exodus 14:10-31; 15:20-21 (Israel's Deliverance at the Red Sea); Isaiah 55:1-11 (Salvation Offered Freely to All); Ezekiel 36:24-28 (A New Heart and a New Spirit); and Ezekiel 37:1-14 (New Life for God's People).

The Book of Common Prayer (1979), 288–91, provides those seven readings along with two other possibilities: Isaiah 4:2-6 (God's Presence in a Renewed Israel); and Zephaniah 3:12-20 (The Gathering of God's People)..

26. Matthew 28:1-10 in Year A; Mark 16:1-8 in Year B; and Luke 24:1-10 in Year C.

27. *United Methodist Book of Worship*, 87. I have discussed these aspects of the Easter Vigil in *Sacraments and Discipleship, Understanding Baptism and the Lord's Supper in a United Methodist Context* (Ashland, TN: OSL, 2013, prev. publ. 2001, Nashville: Discipleship Resources), 49–53.

28. The image of humanity placed in the Garden "to till it and keep it" (Gen. 2:15) deserves extended reflection.

29. *United Methodist Book of Worship*, 373. Compare *Book of Common Prayer* (1979), 288.

30. In this case, Santa Barbara, California, and Seattle, Washington; and I realized that I know people who live in both locations. Campus violence is not, of course, limited to the United States.

31. For a report with video clip, see the Perkins School of Theology website (accessed August 6, 2014): http://www.smu.edu/Perkins/News/News_Archives/Archives%202013/WalkNRoll.

32. *United Methodist Book of Worship*, 374. Compare *Book of Common Prayer* (1979), 289.

33. Wesley wrote, "This was the 'salvation' of God which they 'stood still' to see—by walking forward with all their might!" "The Means of Grace," Sermon 16, in *The Works of John Wesley*, vol. 1, sermons 1, 1–33, ed. Albert C. Outler (Nashville: Abingdon, 1984), 392.

34. *United Methodist Book of Worship* , 92.

35. Ibid., 375.

36. *Book of Common Prayer* (1979), 291.

Chapter Seven: Intercession and the Discernment of the Christian Community

1. See earlier discussion in the introduction, and also *The United Methodist Book of Worship* (Nashville: United Methodist Publishing House, 1992), 24–25.

2. See *The Book of Common Prayer* (New York: Church Hymnal Corporation, 1979), 383.

3. See my *Extending the Table, A Guide for a Ministry of Home Communion Serving* (Nashville: Discipleship Resources, 2009), 23.

4. I invite you to think of other such questions for corporate discernment. For instance, in an article currently under development, I posit this question for the consideration of pastors, church musicians, and their congregations: "How shall we sing together?" or "How shall we make harmony together?" Unpublished manuscript: "Choosing Hymns at McKee and Beyond: Reflections on a Baptismal Paradigm for the Relationship of Pastors and Church Musicians." Beneath the (perhaps) simple task of choosing hymns lies the relational dynamic of the congregation, and that, ultimately, can shape how the church relates to the rest of the world.

5. "Man Dies for Killing Texas Sheriff's Officer," *Dallas Morning News*, March 12, 2010, 4A.

6. Shirl James Hoffman, *Good Game: Christianity and the Culture of Sports* (Waco, TX: Baylor University Press, 2010), 119.

7. Luis Alberto Urrea, *The Devil's Highway* (New York: Little, Brown, 2005).

8. Rebecca Skloot, *The Immortal Life of Henrietta Lacks* (New York: Crown, 2010), 30, 205, 315, 322–25.

9. Tasha Tsiaperas, "Trial Delayed Until December for Man Accused of Killing Kaufman DA, Wife, His Top Assistant," accessed August 14, 2014, http://crimeblog.dallasnews.com/2014/05/trial-delayed-until-december-for-man-accused-of-killing-kaufman-da-wife-his-top-assistant.html/#more-69087.

10. Joyce Rupp, *Walk in a Relaxed Manner: Life Lessons from the Camino* (Maryknoll, NY: Orbis, 2005), 149–50.

11. Our Callings in the World, accessed August 14, 2014, http://www.ourcallingsintheworld.net/.

12. The aforementioned Hillsman Jackson suggests that I could do a similar exercise, asking the students to stand in one place, noticing all that surrounds them and all that passes by.

13. Alyce M. McKenzie, *Novel Preaching: Tips From Top Writers for Crafting Creative Sermons* (Louisville, KY: Westminster/John Knox Press, 2010), 5–6, 15–16, 38.

14. Kenneth W. Stevenson, *To Join Together: The Rite of Marriage* (New York: Pueblo, 1987), 212, 228.

15. *The United Methodist Hymnal* (Nashville: United Methodist Publishing House, 1989), 879.

16. Author's notes on conversation with St. Matthew's United Methodist Church prayer group, January 22, 2012.

17. William W. Eason, "The Danger of Pulling Weeds in God's Garden," unpublished sermon manuscript, March 22, 2011. Used by permission.

18. William B. Lawrence, "Commencement Benediction," Southern Methodist University, May 12, 2012. Reprinted with permission.

19. William B. Lawrence, interview by author, December 14, 2012.

20. Ibid.

21. Ibid.

22. Ibid.

Chapter Eight: So Then, What Difference Does It Make? Toward Some Positive Assertions

1. William B. Lawrence, interview by author, December 14, 2012.

2. For example, the next time a leader is presented with dueling prayer requests, she might acknowledge the conflict and, instead of offering a specific prayer, call the congregation to a moment of silent prayer. In addition, pastors can use various media, sermons, and other conversations to teach toward better practice. One might put the question to the congregation or its representatives, taking a variant on "Why don't we pray for . . . ?" and instead asking, "How shall we pray?"

3. For background on some of this discussion, see the book by Brother Emmanuel of Taizé, as translated by Dinah Livingstone, *Love Imperfectly Known: Beyond Spontaneous Representations of God* (London: Continuum, 2011). On October 31, 2012, it was my

delight to engage in conversation with Brother Emmanuel, along with several Perkins students and faculty members.

4. Paul Shirley, *Can I Keep My Jersey? 11 Teams, 5 Countries, and 4 Years in My Life as a Basketball Vagabond* (New York: Villard, 2007), 289–90, emphasis added.

5. See *Hymns on the Lord's Supper* (1745), hymn 101, from stanzas three and four: "A drop of heaven o'erflows our hearts, and deluges the house of clay . . . the drop shall swell into a sea." J. Ernest Rattenbury, *The Eucharistic Hymns of John and Charles Wesley*, ed. Timothy J. Crouch (Cleveland: OSL, 1990), H-33.

6. Scot Bontrager, unpublished sermon, Profession Service, Order of Saint Luke Perkins chapter, May 15, 2008. E-mail from Scot Bontrager, September 11, 2008, author's file.

7. See my article "Intercessions After the Storm: A Reflection on the Work of Public Intercessions," *Sacramental Life* 17, no. 4 (Fall 2005): 50; and Marjorie Procter-Smith, *Praying with our Eyes Open* (Nashville: Abingdon, 1995), 72–73. See earlier reference in chap. 5.

8. Paul Meyendorff, *The Anointing of the Sick* (Crestwood, NY: St. Vladimir's Seminary Press, 2009), 32.

9. For an excellent discussion of the distinction between healing and cure, and the ways in which confusing the two can cloud our thinking, see the book by Bruce T. Morrill, *Divine Worship and Human Healing: Liturgical Theology at the Margins of Life and Death* (Collegeville, MN: Liturgical Press, 2009), 56, 68, 74–75, 83, etc.

10. *The Book of Offices and Services After the Usage of The Order Of Saint Luke*, ed. Timothy J. Crouch (Cleveland: Order of Saint Luke, 1988), 57–83. See his earlier work in the following volumes: Timothy J. Crouch, ed., *A United Methodist Rite for Anointing* (East Ohio Conference Chapter, Order of Saint Luke, 1980); Crouch, ed., *A United Methodist Rite for Anointing* (Order of Saint Luke, 1986).

11. "A Service of Healing 1," in *The United Methodist Book of Worship* (Nashville: United Methodist Publishing House, 1992), 615–21. See also the introductory material on pp. 613–15.

12. Colette M. Jenkins, "Minister Now Supported by Others' Prayers, Help," *Akron Beacon Journal*, February 16, 2005, A-1.

13. Participant observation at St. James Episcopal Church, Dallas, April 14, 2010; and Marci Pounders, interview by author, February 12, 2010.

14. Pounders interview, February 12, 2010.

15. Marci J. Pounders, "A Tale of Two Deaths: A Palliative Care Chaplain Reflects," *Journal of Palliative Medicine* 12, no. 11 (November 2009): 1057.

16. Ibid., 1057–58.

17. For a fuller account of Marci Pounders' work, see her Doctor of Ministry project thesis: *Ars Moriendi in Praxis: The Effects of a Comprehensive Hospital Bereavement Program on Grieving Patients and Families* (Dallas, TX: Southern Methodist University, 2012).

18. Roberto L. Gómez, interview by author, July 12, 2011; and e-mail to author September 13, 2014.

19. John W. Stamm, "Reflections of a Veteran Retiree," unpublished manuscript for a talk delivered to the banquet for retirees and ordinands at the Central Pennsylvania Conference, meeting at Messiah College, Grantham, Pennsylvania, June 9, 2006.

20. As in the Episcopal Church. *The Book of Common Prayer* (New York: Church Hymnal Corporation, 1979), 308–9.

21. *United Methodist Book of Worship* , 91.

22. Indeed, Laurence Hull Stookey, the key framer and interpreter of the United Methodist Baptismal Covenant rite, insisted that the rubric be written so as to allow congregants to join the pastor in this laying on of hands and blessing. See the discussion in Robert Brian Peiffer's dissertation, *How Contemporary Liturgies Evolve: The Revision of United Methodist Liturgical Texts (1968–1988)* (PhD diss., University of Notre Dame, 1993), 235.

www.ingramcontent.com/pod-product-compliance
Lightning Source LLC
LaVergne TN
LVHW050520201225
827877LV00008B/29
9780881777123